About the Autnor

Sourabh Mukherjee is the author of three psychological thriller novels – *The Sinners, In the Shadows of Death* and *The Colours of Passion*, long-listed in WordToScreen, Mumbai International Film Festival, 2018. He has also written three short story collections along with a bestselling thriller in Bengali, *Chandralekha Nihato*.

An Electronics and Telecommunications Engineer from Jadavpur University, Kolkata, in his day-job, Sourabh works in a senior leadership role in a global technology firm. Sourabh also sits in the Academic Councils of several premier educational institutions in India. He has spoken in global technology summits in London and Las Vegas, as well as at events organized by Bengal Chamber of Commerce and Industry, IIFT, Symbiosis, IIT Guwahati, Kolkata University, IISWBM, Techno India, and University of Engineering & Management, among others.

Sourabh has won several literary awards and recognitions, including Golden Pen Award in the Sulekha Monsoon Romance Contest (2014), Juggernaut Selects (2019), Keynote Speaker in Literoma International Symposium for Literature and Festival (2020). He was awarded the Man of Excellence Award, 2021 by Indian Achievers' Forum for his professional achievements and contributions to nation-building.

www : www.sourabhmukherjee.com   f : authorsourabhmukherjee

Instagram : authorsourabhmukherjee   Twitter : sourabhm_ofcl

By the same author

Novels

The Sinners

In the Shadows of Death

The Colors of Passion

Short story collections

Loves Lost

Beyond 22 Yards

It's All About Love

Bengali thriller

Chandralekha Nihato

Appreciation for the author and his works

"Sourabh Mukherjee has emerged as one of the front-runners in Indian crime fiction over the last five years."

– *Mid-Day*

"Mukherjee has definitely left his mark on the genre."

– *Deccan Herald*

"One of the most popular writers of Indian crime fiction."

– *The Asian Age*

"...is a fast-paced potboiler which hooks you and keeps you glued to the plot from the very beginning."

– *The Times of India*

"With an almost Freudian understanding of how our childhood experiences influence our adult decisions, [In the Shadows of Death] paints a stark picture of urban life in India."

– *The Hindu*

"The theatrical finale comes as much from the extraordinary storytelling as it does from the reveal of the murderer. Mukherjee has the unerring eye of a master craftsman."

– *The Hindu*

"Just when you think you've got it all figured out as per the clues that the killer leaves like crumbs, the author throws you off the path repeatedly with the twists."

– *Business Standard*

"A whodunit with several twists...has elements of romance, corporate scandals, and suspense with a strong emotional undercurrent."

– *The New Indian Express*

"A heady concoction of thrill, mystery, psychology and humanity is what makes [In the Shadows of Death] such an engrossing fare."

– *The Tribune*

"*The Sinners* is a thrilling work of fiction that weaves together elements of corporate warfare and personal vendetta."

– *Yahoo! News*

"A psychological thriller in the true sense of the phrase...delves deep into the psyche of its characters.

– *The Free Press Journal*

"The character of detective Agni Mitra has been rendered in a very believable and realistic fashion. The author has rummaged into the human psyche and used it as the basis for the detective's theories."

– *Tahlka News*

"Mukherjee has explored the materialistic, urban life, its turmoils and fragility of relationships."

– *World News Network*

"*In the Shadows of Death* explores the city of Kolkata in a way few contemporary novels have attempted. The City of Joy is not just a backdrop, but another character in the novel."

– *Go-Getter, Go Air in-flight magazine*

"*The Colours of Passion* is a gripping detective thriller delving into complexities of love and hate, and also into their psychological reasons and motives."

– *The News Now*

"*The Sinners* is definitely the must-read thriller book of the year."

– *The Week*

"*The Sinners* is a gripping and riveting read."

– *Outlook*

DEATH SERVED COLD

INDIA'S MOST DANGEROUS WOMEN MURDERERS

SOURABH MUKHERJEE

Srishti
PUBLISHERS & DISTRIBUTORS

Srishti Publishers & Distributors
A unit of AJR Publishing LLP
212A, Peacock Lane
Shahpur Jat, New Delhi – 110 049
editorial@srishtipublishers.com

First published by
Srishti Publishers & Distributors in 2021

10 9 8 7 6 5 4 3 2

This is a fictionalised narrative based on true crimes that happened in India. The real identity of everyone involved in the cases has been kept under wraps and names of people, places and events have been changed or used fictitiously.

Printed and bound in India

To Mou and Rik.
Love you for keeping me honest,
rooted and adored.

Contents

Prologue

Professor Dutt took a drag of his cigar. Dev Rathee saw the glow at the tip of the cigar get brighter, and then the smoke curled out of the professor's mouth, forming transient patterns around his face.

There were ominous rumblings in the sky. An odd car or two swooshed down the empty road outside the professor's bungalow. The trees that lined the compound wall looked like patches of dark ink against the night sky. There was a dog barking somewhere in the distance.

Professor Dibakar Dutt was an eminent psychologist. In addition to his expertise in clinical psychology and counselling, he also possessed extensive knowledge on the subject of criminal psychology. Dev worked for *The News of India* and his immensely popular column on crime had made him a household name. What his readers were blissfully unaware of were the painfully long hours of investigation and research that went into each of his brilliant pieces. The professor, of course, was the one to whom Dev ran to, every time he needed an insight into the twisted minds of the criminals he routinely wrote about. Dev had recently decided to write about Indian women who had committed heinous murders over the years. He was eager to pick on the brain of the learned professor.

"The idea that a woman can kill, not just with a smile, but also with a knife, is often unacceptable in our society." The professor smiled and continued, "And it is because we have conditioned ourselves to look at women as nurturers over the ages. They selflessly perform the roles of mothers, sisters and wives and are considered to be the embodiments of compassion and kindness. How can they think of taking lives away when they are life-givers themselves? It is rather the tendency of men to be cruel and sadistic. They are more likely to commit despicable crimes."

The professor took a dramatic pause so that Dev could reflect on this popular opinion. Then, he continued further, *"The fact, however, is that gender has nothing to do with the propensity of a human being to commit a crime."*

Dev nodded in agreement, sipping on the *masala chai* that the professor's domestic help made for him every time he visited.

"Professor, is there a pattern that you have observed in the murders that both genders commit? What are the motives which drive them to perform such horrendous acts?" Dev asked.

The professor thought for some time and said, "Quite a few, actually. Men are more likely to kill for sex, sadism and violence, while women kill mostly for money, or to protect their own reputation and integrity. A woman often kills someone to hide an illicit relationship or to get out of one. Lust and greed, however, are common motives for both genders."

Dev made notes in his tab. The professor went on, "Also, statistics from all over the world confirm a few of my personal observations. Women are more likely to kill people they have known for a while, or the ones they have been close to. They also plan their murders more meticulously, often over a period of time. Therefore, it often becomes very difficult to prove their guilt. Sometimes, she may even turn against a partner in crime, in the course of an investigation and is often let off with a lesser punishment by the judiciary."

A pattern was beginning to emerge in Dev's mind as he listened intently to the professor. He further asked, "Professor, is there some geographical or cultural pattern as well? How frequently do you come across a woman committing a gruesome murder in our country?"

The professor stood up. He walked to the cabinet and returned with a couple of thick files.

"Dev, you would be shocked to know how many of these dangerous women I have studied in my long career – all of them from our country. They are all ordinary women; just like someone in your family, or the nice lady who lives next door. But the stories in these files are gruesome. The circumstances, the people involved in the crimes, the timings, the places, the motives – these stories are chilling enough to give you sleepless nights!"

"Professor, if you don't mind, I would like to keep these files with me for a few days. I promise I would return them as soon as I am done writing," Dev requested.

Professor Dutt handed the files over to Dev with a smile.

Later that night, in his study, Dev opened the 'Femme Fatale Files', as he called them. He filtered out cases over a fairly long time horizon, and from different parts of the country.

As he started going through the accounts, he lost track of time. He realized that the good professor had not exaggerated one bit when he had said that those were stories of ordinary women around us whose heinous acts left one shocked, disturbed and scared.

His Last Cry

4 May 2017

Babua sat up on his bed and picked up his mobile phone. He rubbed his eyes and looked at the time. Fifteen minutes to seven. He wondered why Mahua didi was calling him so early.

The sweltering heat had kept Babua up all night. The drowsiness was compelling him to stay in bed for some more time that morning. But that was not to be!

"Babua, what took you so long to pick up?" Mahua sounded impatient at the other end of the line.

"I'm still in bed, didi. Is everything alright?" Babua stifled a yawn.

"I'm sorry I had to call you so early. Please do me a favour, will you? Can you please check on Nirupam? He hasn't called me since last night and I am worried. I called him a few times, but he didn't pick up the phone. I could barely sleep last night."

"Don't worry, didi. Let me check. I will ask him to call you."

Babua stepped out of bed and threw a shirt over his bare and sweat-slick body. He slid his feet into a pair of *chappals* and headed towards the house where Mahua and Nirupam lived. It was about five minutes' walk.

Strictly speaking, Babua was a *mama* (maternal uncle) to Mahua. But, he was younger than her and called her 'didi'. More than anything else, the two were thick friends. Like Mahua, Babua also had a passion for dancing. The two regularly performed in stage shows.

The neighbourhood was already up. There were men sitting on wooden benches in tea stalls and enjoying their morning tea with hot *jalebis* and *samosas*. There were children waiting for their school buses. The heat and the humidity were unbearable, even though it was just about seven in the morning.

When he reached Nirupam's house, Babua called Nirupam by his name. There was no response. He noticed that the small iron gate was open. He walked across the small garden in front of the house. When he reached the main door, he rang the bell and called out, "Nirupam! Where are you?"

He received no response. Babua was about to knock on the door when he realized that the door was open. Babua pushed the door. As he was about to enter, the newspaper hawker rang the bell of his cycle outside the house and the day's newspaper, rolled and tied with a string, landed on the veranda near Babua's feet. It was a perfect aim, like every other day.

Little did Babua know that thirty-six-year-old Nirupam Saha would make it to the headlines of every newspaper the very next morning.

When Babua stepped into the room, his jaw dropped. An involuntary shriek escaped his mouth and he stepped a few inches back. Nirupam was lying in a pool of blood on the floor of the living room. There was blood all over his body and his face had been disfigured. Nirupam had been mercilessly battered, almost ripped apart by his assailant.

Babua rushed out into the garden and collapsed on the ground, feeling breathless. He retched a few times and the world around him was a haze. After a while, when he had managed to regain his senses, Babua stood up and started running towards his house. He had to inform his family and most importantly, Mahua didi.

Twenty-eight-year-old Mahua Tarafdar was inconsolable when she was brought to the scene of crime. Babua had called her, and then gone straight to Mahua's house, as his family had suggested. Babua knew how much Mahua loved her husband.

Only a few months back, on Valentine's Day, the couple had gone on a picnic. They had posted their video on social media, which their friends and families had found to be very romantic and heart-warming. In the video, Mahua and Nirupam could be seen showering accolades on each other. Mahua said that she loved the way Nirupam took care of her and her family, and she knew that Nirupam would do anything to fulfil all her wishes. Nirupam, on the other hand, said that he was thankful to Mahua for the way in which she had adjusted herself to their married life, and how she loved and respected his family.

The video flashed before Babua's eyes as he led Mahua across the garden to her house.

As Mahua stood at the door, looking at the forensics team working on the body of her husband and her house teeming with cops, the memories came flooding back.

Mahua had known Nirupam for more than six years. Simple and soft-spoken, Nirupam owned a travel agency. He also worked in a money exchange firm. Nirupam was originally a resident of Bangladesh. His family still lived there.

While Mahua's family wanted her to get married to Nirupam, Mahua was in no hurry. She wanted to continue with her studies, pursue her passion for dancing and find a job. In the meantime, however, Mahua's parents visited Bangladesh and met Nirupam's family to finalize the alliance. When everything fell into place, Mahua's parents did not want to delay the wedding. Nirupam had been seeing their daughter for more than five years and it was time that the two got married. They did not want tongues wagging in the small town.

When Mahua still did not give her consent, her parents met the local councillor, who was a family friend. He understood Mahua's concern and assured her that he would ensure that she was financially independent. Mahua must, however, fulfil her parents' wishes and get married. In any case, the boy was not a stranger. She had been dating him for more than five years.

Mahua took up the job of a casual staffer in Barasat Municipality, and about a year before Nirupam's gruesome murder, the lovers got married.

Nirupam had no inkling that there was trouble brewing in his paradise.

When Sujit Sen walked into the living room of the Tarafdars, his heart skipped a few beats as he saw Mahua reclining on her favourite armchair, reading a novel. She had not seen him entering the room.

Sujit kept standing at the door, his eyes soaking in the charms of the girl he had fallen in love with, the very first time they had met in college. However, Sujit had always known that Mahua was ambitious. She aspired for a luxurious life, and with his modest roots and meagre earnings, Sujit would never be able to make her happy. Given that, he had chosen to remain 'just good friends' with Mahua, running errands for her and the Tarafdars. He often sneaked in a bottle of vodka for Mahua and finished it with her in the attic. He watched from the wings as Mahua moved from one affluent lover to another. Her search finally ended with Nirupam as she painted the town red with him for more than five years before getting married to him. Mahua was now someone else's wife, way out of his reach. She had visited her parents a few times over the last few months, but Sujit had never met her.

Now twenty-six years old, Sujit had himself married once, but his marriage had not lasted too long. He had tried his best to forget Mahua and get on with his life, but he could not manage to tame his restless heart.

But sometimes, your biggest love turns out to be your biggest mistake.

Mahua looked up from the book to see Sujit and their eyes locked. Sujit's heart thumped so loudly that he was afraid that Mahua would hear it. The fact that Mahua was now another man's wife somehow made her more desirable. As she reclined on the arm chair in a thin sleeveless nightie, the *mangalsutra* buried in her cleavage, her wet hair open with a dash of red *sindoor* in the parting and her voluptuous body flaunting her sexuality, he was suddenly consumed by an unbridled desire to take her in his arms. He yearned to kiss her moist lips, rip her clothes apart and make passionate love.

He came out of his reverie when Mahua finally spoke, "Do you mind coming in if you are done sizing me up?"

Sujit blushed, wondering if his excitement was too evident. He walked in and sat down next to Mahua.

"When did you come?" he asked, gazing at Mahua's lips.

"Last evening." Mahua smiled.

Sujit nodded and asked, "How long are you going to be here?"

"It seems you are in a hurry to see me off!" Mahua faked her anger.

"No, not at all! In fact, it feels great to see you again after so many months," Sujit stuttered. "We never met after your marriage."

"It feels great to see you too." Mahua placed a hand on Sujit's hand, looking into his eyes. Sujit feared that her touch would scald his hand. For the next several minutes, Mahua did not move her hand and held his gaze. The only sound in the room was of their breathing.

After what seemed like blissful eternity, Mahua brought her face close to Sujit's and said, "I will have to leave tonight. But, let us get drunk. Like old times! Can you bring a bottle of vodka in the evening, Sujit?"

Mahua's breath fanned the fire in Sujit's heart. He was confused by the games his mind and the woman in front of him were playing with him.

Mahua and Sujit were on the roof, looking up at the stars in the clear autumn sky. A gentle breeze caressed their faces. The vodka was beginning to kick in and suddenly, the world seemed to be a better place.

Mahua had finished one glass after another in long swigs.

"Why are you in such a hurry?" Sujit asked, looking at Mahua's empty glass. He reached for the bottle of vodka to fill her glass again and said, "You said you won't leave before ten."

"I am parched, Sujit. I haven't had a drink in months," Mahua said.

"Why? Doesn't Nirupam drink?"

"No! No one in his family has ever touched alcohol. They are too virtuous, you see!" Mahua laughed loudly. "...and terribly boring!"

Sujit smiled. "How's life otherwise?" he asked.

"There isn't much going on. Nirupam spends most of his time chasing money. His work keeps him very busy these days." Mahua sighed.

"Well, I thought the two of you are the happiest couple in the world!" Sujit reached inside his pocket and pulled out his mobile phone. He went to Facebook and pulled up a video which Mahua had posted shortly after her marriage.

They had gone to a picnic with friends and colleagues. Mahua could be seen describing Nirupam as the perfect husband. Nirupam said in the video, "I admire Mahua's commitment and strength of character. I will go to any length to fulfil the desires of my beautiful wife and love her till the last day of my life."

Mahua scoffed at the video and said, "Stop believing everything you see on Facebook! The bitter truth is, I'm lonely, Sujit."

Sujit held her hand and the two drank in silence for several minutes.

Finally, Mahua kissed Sujit on the cheek and said, "Thanks for the evening, Sujit. It's so good to have you back in my life."

Am I back in her life? Sujit kept wondering as the two got up to leave.

Nirupam looked at the wall clock when Mahua tottered into the bedroom. "Do you have any idea what time it is?" he asked sternly.

"Nirupam, this is as much my house as it's yours. I don't owe anyone an explanation if I come home late," Mahua slurred.

Nirupam sat up straight, his face flushed in anger.

"Are you… are you drunk?" he asked.

"Yes, I am," Mahua said. "We had a small party at home. I've told you, Nirupam. We aren't prudes, unlike you and your folks," Mahua said, trying to nip this confrontation in the bud.

"What do you mean by *we*?" Nirupam said.

"Now you are doubting me, are you?" Mahua asked angrily.

"All I am asking you is, who have you been drinking with?"

"What else can I expect from you? You make a fuss even if I accept friend requests on Facebook," Mahua was livid. She continued, "If you had your way, you would keep me locked up in this house. You even hate the fact that I work, don't you?"

Nirupam was quiet.

But there was no stopping Mahua. "It was my mistake that I couldn't understand before our marriage that you were so narrow-minded. You are the kind who believes that a woman doesn't deserve to be free. She cannot have a mind of her own..."

Nirupam cut her off and said, "Mahua, you are taking this too far! You have all the freedom you deserve."

"You don't love me anymore, Nirupam. All you want from me now is a baby," Mahua said, dejected.

"Don't bring that up, Mahua! We talked about it. I would love to have a baby and we aren't getting any younger."

"And didn't I tell you that I need more time? But, all you want me to do is stay at home and make babies for you. Of course, when we get some time off from entertaining *your* visitors from Bangladesh."

"Shut up, Mahua! The ones you call visitors are my family—"

"—that cannot get enough of Barasat and makes sure that someone or the other from Bangladesh is in this house every week," Mahua interrupted him.

"You are pathetic!" Nirupam raised his voice a notch.

"Is it? If you think that I'm pathetic, why don't you pick up the phone and complain to dad? That's what you always do behind my back, don't you? And I have to sit through dad's lectures every time I go home."

Mahua stormed out of the room, muttering to herself, "It's disgusting that my parents think just like you do. Every time I leave you, they push me back to this hell."

"Sujit, I can't live without you," Mahua said, her head on Sujit's bare chest, his heart beating in her ears. He kissed her on the head, his fingers lost in her tresses. Mahua snuggled closer, pressing her bare body against his. Sujit pulled her closer, and they kissed.

Nirupam was out conducting one of his tours and Sujit had stayed back for the night. There was a bottle of vodka which was two-thirds empty, a bottle of Limca, a few packs of crisps and two empty glasses on the nightstand. Mahua and Sujit never missed the chance to be with each other, every time Nirupam went on his tours.

"Do you love me?" Sujit looked into Mahua's eyes and asked.

"Do you still doubt me?" Mahua asked in return.

"All of this feels like a dream, Mahua. This is what I always wanted. I fell in love with you when we were in college. But I was always aware of your ambitions. To be honest with you, I never considered myself worthy of you..."

Mahua put a hand on Sujit's mouth and shut him up.

"What makes you say that?" she asked.

"Why would you want to be with someone like me? I struggle to earn my daily bread," he responded.

"Do you really believe that I would choose to be with someone only for his money?" Mahua asked.

Sujit did not reply.

Mahua went on, "Nirupam does make a lot of money. My parents almost forced me to marry him. But he has no time for me. I feel suffocated when he is around. All the money in the world cannot change that. So what if I am the nominee for all his money? So what if all his property would be mine someday? I will not get the best years of my life back!"

Mahua started sobbing. Sujit pulled her closer.

He could not help wondering how much Mahua would be worth if Nirupam were to die. The two of them would never have to worry about money.

Mahua smiled to herself. She knew exactly what Sujit was thinking. The seed had been sown.

As soon as Sujit stepped out of the neighbourhood club, a motorbike stopped in front of him. Sujit had been in the club playing cards with his friends and hence, he was late for dinner.

The man on the bike removed his helmet. It was Nirupam. He was the last person Sujit had expected to see.

"Nirupam, what a surprise! How are you doing?"

"Sujit, I went to your house and was told that I would find you in the club."

"Yes, I usually come here in the evenings," Sujit replied, getting slightly nervous.

Nirupam said with a smirk, "That is when you are not in my house fucking my wife."

Sujit felt like he had been punched in his gut.

"It doesn't take too long for word to get around our town, Sujit," said Nirupam. "I know what Mahua and you are up to these days. I have been suspicious for a long time, and now I know for sure."

Sujit stood rooted to the spot, his head bowed. From the corner of his eye, he saw some of his friends watching them from inside the club.

Nirupam brought his face close to Sujit's and said, "Stay away from my wife, Sujit! I'm warning you."

Nirupam put his helmet on, started his bike and rode off into the night.

Sujit stood there, seething in anger, his fists balled up.

After a few minutes, he called Mahua.

"Missing me?" Mahua took the call after the first ring.

"Nirupam knows," Sujit said. "He met me just now and threatened me with dire consequences if we don't stop meeting."

There was silence for a few seconds at the other end of the line.

Then Mahua whispered into the phone, "In that case, his time is up."

"What do you mean?" Sujit wanted to confirm if Mahua really meant what he thought she meant.

"I have enough money in my joint account with Nirupam to hire someone to finish him off," Mahua said, before ending the call.

Sujit kept looking unbelievingly at the phone. Mahua's words had made his heart skip a beat.

3 May 2017

Mahua rushed to the door when she heard the bell.

She had called Sujit for a secret rendezvous in the afternoon. She had left work early, feigning sickness. It did not bother Mahua that the Municipality had already served her a show cause notice for her irregular attendance. Mahua had lost interest in the job. She had a plan that would make her wealthy in a matter of few days. Of course, she needed Sujit's help to carry out that plan.

As soon as Sujit entered the house, Mahua pounced on him like a famished tigress. They fumbled at each other's clothes and in no time, were all over each other inside the bedroom. As Mahua guided Sujit inside her to ride him, it seemed to him that something had come over her. Straddling him, she moved in rhythm with his thrusts, her nails clawing his chest, her throaty moans reverberating in the empty house.

Mahua's phone rang. She looked at it from the corner of her eye. It was Babua. They had been planning a dance show together. Even as she bobbed up and down, breathing hard, Mahua picked up the phone and rejected the call.

When Mahua finally collapsed on Sujit, he was exhausted, yet ready for an encore. He had never experienced such ecstatic pleasure and flipped her over. Pinning her to the bed, he was ready to mount her, when Mahua pushed him away.

"What's the matter, sweetheart?" Sujit whispered into her ears.

Mahua looked into his eyes and said, "I want you to do something for me."

"What is it?" Sujit asked impatiently.

"I want you to kill Nirupam. For me. For us," Mahua said, kissing Sujit so hard that she drew blood from his lower lip.

"I thought we were going to hire a killer!" Sujit sounded surprised.

"Why waste money when my tiger can do it by himself," Mahua kissed Sujit once again.

"I'll do anything for you," Sujit said.

"Then, listen to me very carefully. We need to do it today. Here is the plan…"

After she had explained her plan to Sujit, Mahua called Babua.

She whispered into the phone, "Babua, I'm in a meeting right now. I'll call you when I'm back home."

Babua heard from Mahua again the next morning, when she asked him to check on Nirupam.

Mahua had not been keeping well over the last few days, and now her sudden decision of going away to her parents' place made Nirupam all the more worried. As he ended the day and left his office, Nirupam called Mahua once again.

"Are you sure you're alright?" he asked.

"Yes, I'm absolutely fine. Stop worrying about me. Go home and get some rest. You've been working too hard."

They had spoken on the phone several times since afternoon. In every conversation, Mahua had repeatedly told him that she was fine and Nirupam did not have to go all the way to his in-laws' place to see her. She would be back home soon.

Having finally convinced Nirupam not to visit her, Mahua called Sujit.

"Be ready. He's on his way home. I don't think he's too far."

Sujit ended the call and made sure that all the lights inside the house were switched off. He walked to the living room and stood against the wall by the main door. Mahua had locked him inside the house before leaving for her parents' place. She had originally wanted to stay back and then, the two had decided that it was better that she stayed away from the scene, as it would be too risky otherwise.

Sujit tightened his grip on the iron rod when he heard footsteps in the veranda. That must be Nirupam, he thought. He took out his phone and dialled Mahua's number. As she received the call, Sujit transferred the phone to a pocket in his trousers.

Mahua had asked Sujit to call her on her alternate mobile number so that she could hear the last cries of her husband as he died.

Sujit could hear Nirupam stop in front of the main door, and then the jangle of keys. The lock clicked open. Nirupam pushed the door and stepped in. As Nirupam fumbled his way inside the dark living room, Sujit swung the iron rod and hit Nirupam on the back of his head. Nirupam screamed and fell down. Sujit quickly closed the door from inside and continued to batter Nirupam with the iron rod.

As Nirupam cried out in pain, begging for mercy, Sujit checked if Mahua was still at the other end of the line. He wanted to make sure that Mahua was relishing the macabre broadcast of the excruciating and agonizing last moments of her husband.

When Nirupam could barely move, Sujit sat down on his knees and pulled the knife out from the back pocket of his trousers. He started randomly slashing the hapless man who was writhing on the floor in a pool of blood. Nirupam's end was near, and he made one last attempt to cry for help. As soon as he opened his mouth, Sujit thrust the iron rod inside his mouth and cracked his jaw open.

He pulled out the phone and brought it near Nirupam's mouth, so that Mahua could hear Nirupam wail in the last few minutes of his life. She had wanted to see Nirupam die, which the two had decided against. This was the closest she could get to that spectacle.

When Sujit was sure that Nirupam was dead, he pulled Nirupam's engagement ring off his finger. Mahua had wanted it back. He transferred the ring to a pocket and went to the bathroom. He turned on the shower and stood under it, as the ice-cold water washed Nirupam's blood off his body. He then, went to the washbasin and rinsed as much of the blood off his trousers as he could manage to. Finally, he dried himself, put on his shirt and left the house.

"Meet me after you've finished the job," Mahua had told him. Sujit headed for Mahua's house to return the engagement ring.

He would then have to run away for a while. Run away from himself.

Later that night, Sujit went to Shobhabazar and drank endlessly. His next stop was Sonagachi, where he spent the night with a hooker. The next morning, he went to Dakshineswar and took a dip in the Hooghly. He threw away into the river the clothes he had worn while killing Nirupam, which he had stuffed into a plastic bag as soon as he had reached home last night. He also got rid of one of Nirupam's mobile phones.

However, Sujit could not silence the clamour inside his head.

The police considered several possibilities when investigations started.

Nirupam's murder might have been due to a family feud. There might have been conflicts or disagreements with his business rivals, colleagues or partners. Or, Nirupam might have been murdered as he had resisted an attempted robbery. The last possibility was summarily rejected by the police as there was no *prima facie* indication of robbery. As the police spoke to Nirupam's colleagues, they realized that the second possibility could also be ruled out, as there was no evidence of conflict with co-workers or business rivals. That left the investigators with the first option as the most likely one.

Sujit came on the radar of the investigators when they started going through Mahua's call records. The number of calls and messages exchanged between Sujit and Mahua over the last few months clearly indicated that the two were more than just ex-classmates. The police then looked into the call records of Sujit.

The location details of Sujit's phone revealed that he had been at the scene of crime since the afternoon till late into the night. He had then gone to Mahua's house, then to Shobhabazar, and had spent the rest of the night in the red-light area in Sonagachi. After which, he had gone to Dakshineswar. Sujit's movements on the day of the crime perplexed the police. They questioned him again and again.

It also turned out that at the time of the crime, Sujit had made a call to a number for several minutes. The police found out that the number belonged to Mahua Tarafdar. It was an alternate number that she did not use too often, but it was a number registered in her name. The arms of the law were slowly, but surely, catching up with Mahua.

The police needed more evidences.

Then, two interesting details emerged. Firstly, the loss of Nirupam's engagement ring. And secondly, the disappearance of Nirupam's mobile phones.

The investigators came to know that Nirupam always wore his engagement ring. This was confirmed by everyone in his family, his co-workers, as well as some of his neighbours who knew him closely. Nirupam had never parted with that ring, ever since his engagement with Mahua. His co-workers and some of the neighbours whom Nirupam had met on the day of his murder were certain that they had seen the ring on his finger, even on that fateful day.

However, the ring was not found on the body of the victim. Instead, there was a mark on his finger, where the skin was lighter. That was the kind of mark that is left behind when someone removes a ring that has been worn for a very long time. The skin naturally darkens around the ring.

But then, where was Nirupam's engagement ring?

The investigators left no stone unturned, and finally, the ring was found to be in the possession of Mahua. How could Mahua get hold of the ring, when as per her own statement, she had left for her parents' house much before Nirupam had returned home that evening? She had gone back to her house only the next morning, escorted by Babua, when Nirupam had already died and the police had arrived at the scene of crime.

The police had verified from the location details of Mahua's phone that she was at her parents' place all through the evening and night, till the next morning. Therefore, the only explanation could be that the murderer had removed the ring from Nirupam's finger and handed it over to her. The police tallied this theory with the pattern of Sujit's movement that night, and the pieces of the puzzle began to fall into place.

And, where were Nirupam's mobile phones?

The police came to know that Nirupam used two mobile phones, one of which had been gifted to him by Mahua herself. On questioning Sujit, the police came to know that while Sujit had thrown away one of the phones into the Hooghly in the morning after the crime, when he had visited Dakshineswar, the other was still in his possession. The police confiscated the phone immediately. Forensic examination of the phone revealed vital clues regarding the strained relationship of Nirupam and Mahua, a stark contrast to the façade of happy matrimony that the couple had put up for months on social media. The police also saw that Mahua had spoken to Nirupam many times that day, possibly urging him to return home and not visit her parents' place. But, she had left a killer waiting for Nirupam at home.

Sujit started breaking under pressure as he was subjected to multiple rounds of interrogation. As he made his confessions, the police started verifying facts. The police took the lovers to the scene of crime to reconstruct the incidents of that day. Blood, fingerprints and hair samples collected from the scene of crime had already been sent for forensics and DNA tests.

Now, the only piece of the puzzle that was left to be fitted was the motive of the killer. *Why would Mahua want to murder Nirupam?*

There could be three possible theories. First, while the couple pretended to be made for each other, Mahua was unhappy and wanted to break free. The decision to finish off Nirupam might have been an impulsive one, triggered by an argument they might have had on the day of the crime.

Second, Mahua wanted to get married to her long-time lover Sujit and wanted Nirupam out of the way. Sujit mentioned during interrogation that Mahua had always been ambitious and aspired for a life of comfort and luxury. With his meagre earnings from odd jobs, he would have never been able to give Mahua the kind of life she had dreamt of. Nirupam, on the other hand, earned well. So, there had to be a third possibility.

The third and the most realistic theory was that Mahua wanted to get rich, and fast. She was the registered nominee for Nirupam's bank accounts and his properties. Nirupam's death would see his possessions passing on to Mahua, who could then, live a life of affluence with her lover, Sujit.

Finally, about two weeks after the crime, the police arrested Mahua and Sujit.

When the police took Mahua away, Babua was out of town, performing at an event. When he received the news, he could not believe his own ears.

As Babua now remembered Mahua's behaviour during the days after Nirupam's death – quiet and aloof, crying her heart out now and then, he shivered. He could not believe that there was a scheming, cunning murderer lurking inside the woman he called didi, and whom he had been trying to console for two weeks. He had seen how Mahua had seemingly been shattered after Nirupam's death.

On his family's suggestion, he had stayed with Mahua in her parents' house, right from the day of Nirupam's death till two days before her arrest. Babua remembered that all those months since her marriage, there had been instances when Mahua had told him about her fights with Nirupam. Babua had thought such tiffs were common among newlyweds. If he had even the slightest idea that Mahua would plan her husband's murder, he would have talked her out of it. Babua wondered if he would ever be able to trust anyone, even if that person was someone from his own family.

In police custody, while Mahua turned out to be rather indifferent and non-cooperative, Sujit cracked easily. He did not deny his movements as inferred by the police from his mobile phone locations. Mahua had also visited the Kali temple at Dakshineswar with her lover and offered prayers after Nirupam's murder. Whether it was to atone for her sins, or because she had managed to successfully execute her plan of killing her husband, the genuine reason was best known to the lady herself.

In the chargesheet filed after about twelve weeks of the murder, the police charged Mahua under Section 109 of the Indian Penal Code (IPC), in addition to several other charges, including the planning of Nirupam's murder, provocation, helping the execution, misleading the investigators and being responsible for the disappearance of material evidences.

She had acted like a seasoned criminal and was the mastermind behind the gruesome murder, though it was her lover Sujit who had actually carried out the heinous crime. Since there was no eyewitness, the police relied mainly on mobile call records, location details, circumstantial evidence, statements of the accused and forensic reports to build the case. Also, more than two dozen witnesses deposed in the case.

Mahua remained unperturbed and remorseless all through the proceedings. In fact, on the day she was produced in court, when a crowd gathered outside and started hurling abuses at her, she calmly enquired what the fuss was all about!

During her second remand, Mahua tried the last trick up her sleeve. As realization dawned on her that the police had cracked the case, and her doom was imminent, she surprised the investigating officer by offering to become a witness for the state, and by demanding that her lover Sujit be hanged for the murder of her husband. Mahua had thought that this strategic move would be her ticket to freedom. However, to her misfortune, the investigating team confirmed that she would not be allowed to turn state witness against her paramour, as she was the prime accused in the case.

The fast track court in Barasat passed its judgement after the trial ran for close to two years, based on the police chargesheet, mobile phone records and statements of more than thirty witnesses. Mahua and Sujit were found guilty under IPC Section 302 (murder) and Section 120B (criminal conspiracy).

Nirupam's family was disappointed with the verdict. They had expected nothing short of a death sentence.

"I want extreme punishment for the accused. They took away my only son. It should deter others from such sinister designs in future," said Nirupam's father, who had come down to the court from Bangladesh.

"I never saw any remorse in Mahua's eyes in the past two years." That was what hurt Nirupam's mother even more.

To Sir with Love

Fifteen-year-old Sutapa looked at the wall clock one more time. It was almost six in the evening.

Looking outside the window, she could see that the streetlights had come up. Daylight was slowly fading away. Sutapa could see birds forming strange patterns on the purple sky as they flew back to the safety and comfort of their nests.

Sutapa wondered what it was like to call a place one's 'home'. That house, where she lived, could hardly be called one. How could she consider it her home when she lacked the privilege to listen to her heart, the freedom to live and love the way she wanted to?

Sutapa quickly swept her thoughts aside and rushed to the full-length mirror. He would soon be here. Little had Sutapa realized a few months back, when she had started taking private tuitions from Ranbir sir, that he would become the only reason for her to look forward to a new day.

With his pleasant arrival, life was suddenly drenched in the brightest of colours. There was music wafting in the air and her heart throbbed with the fervour of first love, every time Sutapa thought about Ranbir. She thought about him when it rained and the earth smelt sweet. She whispered his name as she fell asleep every night, hugging her pillow tight.

Sutapa brushed her hair and looked at herself in the mirror, turning sideways to check if her breasts were accentuated by the tight tee. She gave them a gentle upward push so that there was more than a hint of a cleavage visible. She felt fire surging through her veins when she remembered the desire she saw in Ranbir's eyes every time he looked at her breasts. Her skirt reached just below her knees. Sutapa closed her eyes, imagining the warmth of Ranbir's hand on her thigh under the study desk. Her pulse raced and she had goose bumps all over. Her ears felt warm and her lips were parched.

She often wished she had a friend with whom she could share the most beautiful secret of her life. After all, she was in love! God had finally been kind to her and she had found a man who was willing to listen to her. Ranbir did not judge her when she told him about how badly her mother treated her, and that she felt like a prisoner in her own house. Sutapa had never had friends. Her mother had never allowed her to step out of the confines of her house. Ranbir had come into her life like a whiff of fresh air.

Sutapa got to spend an hour with Ranbir in her study every evening. But to her, it seemed as if her entire day had been crammed into that hour. She was her own master for that one hour. She could unapologetically be the hapless teenager who was often misunderstood by the world. She could share her grief with the man she loved and have her pain assuaged by his words of compassion. She also felt like the sultry seductress who could turn her charms on to make her lover shed his inhibitions. Her lover touched her and caressed her as she lost herself to sensations she had never known. She loved being attractive and vulnerable at the same time. Maybe, that was what Ranbir loved about her too.

Sutapa was roused from her reverie by the sound of the calling bell.

Her heart skipped a beat. That must be him!

Subodh Mitra lived in Barrackpore with his wife Sujata, his only daughter Sutapa, and his parents Lalita Mitra and Manabendra Mitra. The family was financially well-off and when it came to his daughter's education, Subodh never cut corners. When Sutapa started going to high school, Subodh engaged private tutors for his daughter. Sutapa did not disappoint her father either. She was one of the brightest students in her school. Subodh was proud of his daughter and was certain that Sutapa would grow up to be a smart and self-sufficient woman, who would take care of her family on her own terms.

However, Sutapa had a strained relationship with her mother. Sujata always wanted a boy, and when Sutapa was born, she made no attempt to hide her disappointment. To add to her woes, Sujata ran into several chronic health issues right after Sutapa's birth, which made her irritable. Poor Sutapa was the one on whom Sujata began to vent all her frustration and anger.

Sutapa was not allowed to step out of the house. Sujata would raise hell if she found her daughter talking to a boy. Sutapa was not allowed to make friends even with girls of her age. Sujata would pull her daughter up for the slightest of lapses and would not hesitate to beat her up on some pretext or the other. If Sutapa's father tried to speak for her, he was shouted down too. The fact that Sutapa did not have a friend meant that her anger and her sadness remained bottled up in the deepest recesses of her heart. With every passing day, Sutapa moved further away from her mother.

When Sutapa was promoted to the ninth standard, Subodh engaged the fifty-one-year-old Ranbir Roy to help Sutapa with a few subjects. He was a well-respected teacher in a nearby school. Initially, Sutapa used to visit Ranbir's house where the teacher ran a tutorial centre with several students. However, after some time, with Subodh's permission, Ranbir started teaching Sutapa at her house.

Ranbir started visiting Sutapa four days every week. Before long, Sutapa could sense that it was not just her clever answers that impressed her teacher. The difference in their ages notwithstanding, Ranbir soon became the friend that Sutapa had never had. She started sharing her misery with him, and he listened to her patiently, consoling her with words of compassion.

"You have a bright future, and you should not let anything or anyone come in the way of your success," Ranbir would say, filling Sutapa's eyes with dreams she had never dared to see. She pined for Ranbir's company every moment of the day. Soon, she realized that her life would be incomplete without him. It did not matter to her that Ranbir was married. For the first time in her life, Sutapa was in love, and life had never looked more beautiful.

It was a monsoon evening in 1990. The rumbles in the sky sounded ominous. It was raining, the dirt and grime on the roads washed off.

Sutapa was with Ranbir in her study. She kept looking at the table, silently shedding tears, even as Ranbir explained complex theorems of geometry, wondering all the time why his student had not looked at him for once all through the evening. Ranbir did not know that earlier in the afternoon, Sutapa's mother had seen her talking to the boy next door on her way home from school and had slapped her so hard that

Sutapa had a swelling at the corner of her upper lip, which she was trying to hide from Ranbir.

"Are you alright?" Ranbir finally kept the book down and asked.

Sutapa nodded silently.

"Look at me," said Ranbir.

Sutapa kept looking at the table. Ranbir could see her shoulders shaking. She was crying.

"What's the matter?" Ranbir placed a hand on Sutapa's cheek. He could feel the warmth of her tears on his hand.

Sutapa looked up, and her eyes met Ranbir's.

Ranbir's eyes went to the swelling on her lip.

"What the hell! How did you get *that*?" he asked, slowly moving his thumb over the swelling on Sutapa's lip. There was the sound of loud thunder as the rains lashed against the windows, the water running down the glass panes.

Like a leaf kissed by the first rains of the monsoon, Sutapa's body trembled. She closed her eyes, feeling almost breathless, even as tears rolled down her cheeks. Ranbir kept moving his thumb back and forth on her lips. Sutapa could almost hear the drumming of her heart. The only other sounds were the raindrops on the window and the humming of the electric fan. Sutapa did not want that finger to leave her lips, and almost instinctively, she clutched at Ranbir's hand. Time, it seemed, had stopped. Every inch of her body craved for the warmth of Ranbir's touch.

Sutapa came back to her senses when she heard footsteps and the rustle of her mother's saree outside the room. Ranbir quickly removed his thumb, still looking into Sutapa's eyes, and picked up the book.

That was the beginning. That evening, Sutapa and Ranbir had discovered a whole new way of expressing their feelings for each other – through the language of touch.

In the evenings to follow, Ranbir's hand would find its way to Sutapa's back in a gesture of appreciation or empathy, as the situation demanded. It would stay there more than just a wee bit longer, his fingers pressing deeper into her soft flesh, sending waves of ecstasy down her back. On other evenings, Sutapa would scribble sweet nothings on Ranbir's arm with her nails, the warmth of her closeness and the smell of her body fanning the smouldering embers of his desire.

A whole new world of unknown pleasures was opening up before Sutapa, beckoning her with the lure of the forbidden, although she could barely make sense of her feelings.

"You will find all your answers in books," Ranbir winked as he reached into his bag one evening. Instead of the textbooks of mathematics, he brought out a book with pages that were worn out and dog-eared. As he turned the cover page, Sutapa read the name of the book – *Lolita*. Sutapa had never heard of that book, but as Ranbir read it to her, she was transported to a world ruled by unbridled passion. That book was soon followed by *Lady Chatterley's Lover*, and then *The Kama Sutra* with its graphic pictures.

As Ranbir read from the books, sitting across from Sutapa with the small table between them, he could sense her arousal, her breasts heaving with her heavy breathing and the colour rising in her cheeks. Sometimes, they held hands under the table as Ranbir read. Sometimes Sutapa, craving for his touch, took his hand and placed it on her bare thigh under her dress.

Before long, it became impossible for Sutapa to keep waiting the entire day to be with Ranbir for an hour in the evening. They started meeting during the day. Sutapa bunked classes and Ranbir was absent in school on most days. They hung around in the city, throwing caution to the wind. They would often end up in a movie hall, grabbing corner seats and devouring each other's bodies for the entire duration of the movie.

Sutapa was on an emotional rollercoaster; excited and exhilarated in one moment, but desperate and unsure in the other. Ranbir was now her addiction, but he had a family of his own. There was no way Sutapa could let go of her fix. She had to find a way to ensure that Ranbir would never leave her.

Sutapa knew that Ranbir was not well-off. Moreover, as the two began spending more and more time with each other, on most days Ranbir was absent from duty in the school where he taught. His monthly wages kept dwindling because of the deductions on account of his absence. Sutapa eyed an opportunity and started providing financial assistance to Ranbir, making him obliged to her in the process.

It started with Sutapa talking to her father and securing a loan of six thousand rupees for Ranbir. A couple of months later, when she again approached her father for a loan to help out Ranbir, her father declined. Over the next several weeks, Sutapa secretly handed over her own gold ornaments to Ranbir. It took Sutapa's mother several weeks to find out that a golden chain, which Sutapa wore on special occasions, had gone missing. One afternoon, when Sutapa returned from school with her ring missing, she told her mother that she had lost it in the school playground. Sutapa's mother beat her black and blue, but she bore the pain with a smile. That was but a small price to pay for the success of her grand plan. Sutapa also stole money from her parents for Ranbir.

With every such act of charity, Sutapa was only tightening the noose of debt around Ranbir's neck. There was no way Ranbir could now end his relationship with her and go back to being a devoted husband. Sutapa had managed to buy Ranbir's unflinching loyalty.

It was an autumn evening in September. Ranbir had spent a long and exhausting day and when he reached Sutapa's house on the evening, he had a splitting headache. Sutapa asked him to lie down on the couch. She sat next to him, and taking his head on her lap, she applied a balm and started giving him a relaxing head massage.

Sutapa's mother usually spent her evenings in her room on the ground floor of the house. But as luck would have it, she came up to the first floor on that evening on an errand. Hearing voices inside, she looked into Sutapa's bedroom and was shocked beyond her wits by the scene being played out there. As Sujata stormed into the room, Ranbir got up in a flash and stood with his head bowed.

"How dare you try to seduce a man who is old enough to be your father? Aren't you ashamed?" Sujata grabbed her daughter by her hair and started slapping her in blind fury. Ranbir wanted to speak in Sutapa's defence, but he never managed to open his mouth. Sujata was beside herself with rage, and there was no stopping her.

"My mother doesn't want to see me happy," Sutapa told Ranbir the next time they met. "In fact, she doesn't even want me to do well in my studies. Why else would she want me to stop taking tuitions from you?"

Ranbir took Sutapa's hand in his and nodded in agreement. "What are you going to do about it?" he asked.

"I will kill her," Sutapa said, without batting an eye. She thought for a while and said, "I'd ask Baba to take us to a hill station during the holidays. I'd take *maa* to the top of a hill and then, all it'd take is a gentle push when no one's looking."

Ranbir looked unbelievingly at Sutapa. The fire he saw in her eyes sent a chill down his spine.

"That's quite a fantastic idea." Ranbir smiled wryly.

"Don't smile! I am serious. Tell me if you have a better plan," Sutapa said, her eyes wide in excitement.

Ranbir thought for some time and said, "There is a better

plan, actually. You wouldn't have to wait for your father to take the family to a hill station."

"What do you have in mind?" asked Sutapa.

"You could simply take a whole lot of sleeping pills, crush them into a powder and mix it with the water she drinks at bedtime," Ranbir said. "She wouldn't live to see the next morning!"

Sutapa's lips curled into a crooked smile.

She leaned forward and said, almost in whispers, "Can you get me the pills?"

Ranbir looked into her eyes and nodded.

Three days later, he handed her a small bottle filled with a white powder. "Fifty Calmpose tablets from five different pharmacies," Ranbir whispered. "This should do the trick."

A week later, Sutapa returned the bottle to Ranbir.

"This is not a good idea. The water is in the kitchen, and Maa spends most of her time there. Even when she's not around, there are servants who are present there all the time. It's too risky. Also, we all drink the same water so I can't poison it. We'll all die. I tried one whole week to find a way, but this idea won't work," Sutapa said.

Ranbir took the bottle back. He would have to get rid of the powder at the earliest.

"How else can we poison her?" Sutapa asked in a matter-of-fact manner.

"Let me think of another way," Ranbir said.

Over the next several weeks, Sutapa kept pestering Ranbir to think of other ways to kill her mother. Ranbir kept coming up with ideas and supplying her with different kinds of poison, but she could not muster the courage to carry out her malicious plans. On one such occasion, Ranbir gave her a bottle of water which he had boiled with a lizard. It would have been an infallible recipe for death. But, Sutapa could not find a way to make her mother drink the water from that bottle.

By now, Ranbir's financial situation had improved due to the support provided by Sutapa, who had made sure that Ranbir could not think of leaving her. The lure of sex and money was irresistible. Ranbir started reading chemistry books to discover poisonous chemicals that could be procured easily.

In the meantime, Ranbir's wife Tanuja got wind of her husband's affair with his fifteen-year-old student. Ranbir had been too careless. He had been seen with Sutapa by many of the neighbours at unusual places at odd hours. Tongues started wagging, and before long, the news of his affair reached his wife's ears.

On a cold morning in January, Tanuja knocked on the door of the Mitra residence. Sujata was surprised to see Tanuja at her door so early in the day. But she was not in the least prepared for what happened next. Tanuja launched into a tirade against the Mitras and called Sutapa a 'slut', accusing her of having an illicit relationship with the father of her children. Sujata's doubts were confirmed. It was not just her daughter trying to seduce her tutor, but the two were having an affair. A crowd had assembled in front of the Mitra residence. Sujata had nothing to say to protect the honour of either her daughter or the family. All that Sujata could do was to lock herself up inside her room and pray for the ordeal to get over.

Later that afternoon, as Sutapa lay on her bed, aching all over from the thrashing she had received from her mother, her father entered the room.

"Here, eat something!" He laid down a bowl of rice and dal in front of Sutapa. "You don't have to starve yourself to death. You know what you've done is wrong."

Sutapa bit her lips, trying to stop her tears. She sat up straight with a lot of effort and held her father's hands. "Baba, I know what we've done is not right. But please don't ask sir to stop teaching me. My examinations are only a couple of months away, and I need his guidance. I promise, I'll concentrate only on my studies, but I need his help to do well. You know how important these examinations are for me. We won't find another tutor at such a short notice."

Sutapa coaxed her father into yielding to her wishes. But she realized that she could not wait any longer to kill her mother.

Ranbir had figured out from the chemistry books that there were a number of poisons like Potassium or Sodium Cyanide, Arsenic, Mercuric Chloride, Potassium Permanganate that could be procured from a dealer of chemicals. He found out that his school bought supplies for the laboratory from Dibyendu Basu who ran a business under the name of Scientronic India in the College Row area of Kolkata and dealt in chemicals. When Sutapa heard this, she told Ranbir that they should meet Dibyendu.

When the two reached the store, Ranbir asked Sutapa to wait outside, while he went to meet Dibyendu in his office. Sutapa could see the two through a glass window. She had already asked Ranbir not to negotiate too hard, if Dibyendu asked for money. They needed the poisons at the earliest.

After about half an hour, Ranbir came out of Dibyendu's office. He looked happy. He had managed to strike a deal and Dibyendu had given him some samples. He would test them first on rats before they tried them on Sutapa's mother. Two days later, Ranbir met Sutapa and reported that the samples were adulterated. They had had no effect on the rats. So, the two went back to Dibyendu.

This time, he asked for more time, and the following week, he gave Ranbir the poisons he needed – Sodium Cyanide and Mercuric Chloride.

Given the track record of Dibyendu, Sutapa took no chances, and wanted to test the supplies by herself. She pleaded with her father to get her two guinea pigs. Her parents were surprised by her rather uncharacteristic wish, but then, she was a lonely fifteen-year-old girl who spent her days at home all by herself. So, there was no harm in getting her a couple of pets to spend her time with. Sujata felt that it might also help take her mind off that lecherous tutor. Maybe that was what her daughter wanted as well.

Before long, the Mitras bought two guinea pigs – one snowy white, and the other, white with black patches. They would scurry around all over the house, keeping the Mitras on their toes. One could not but fall in love with them when one looked at their black, beady eyes. However, in less than fourteen days, they were dead. No one but Sutapa knew why and how.

When Sutapa saw the guinea pigs dead, she was thrilled. The poisons had worked.

Next, it would be her mother.

20 March 1991

Sutapa and Ranbir spent the day together, right from ten in the morning to the afternoon. Throughout the day, the two discussed their sinister plan. Sutapa knew that she had to be strong to carry out the plan, else, she would spend the rest of her life in regret. Sutapa went back home around four in the afternoon.

Ranbir reached the Mitra residence at half-past six in the evening. He brought with him sweets for the family – five *kaala-jamuns* and a hundred grams of a local delicacy *sitabhog*. Ranbir went upstairs and Sutapa took the boxes from him. She pierced each and every kaala-jamun and put Sodium Cyanide and Mercuric Chloride inside. She also mixed up the poisons with the sitabhog. Finally, she added Mercuric Chloride to a glass of water and kept it on the study desk.

At around eight in the evening, Sutapa called out for her mother. Sujata had come out from the washroom a while back after taking a shower. Sutapa's father had gone out on an errand and her grandparents were on the ground floor.

When Sujata came upstairs, Ranbir told her that he was sorry about everything that the family had had to go through because of him. He had brought some sweets for the family which was his way of apologizing. He added that he would be very happy if Sujata kindly accepted the sweets. Sutapa, in the meantime, had put two kaala-jamuns on a plate and offered to her mother.

"There was no need for all this," Sujata said nonchalantly, reluctant to pick up the sweets.

"Please Maa, have at least one," Sutapa said, stealing a glance at Ranbir. "Sir would feel very happy. I'd be happy." Ironically, she was honest in her deceit.

Sujata hesitantly picked up one kaala-jamun from the plate and finished it in a hurry, eager to leave the room. "Thank you, Maa," Sutapa smiled and handed her the glass filled with poisoned water. Sujata drank from the glass. Within seconds, she fell down, never to rise again.

Sutapa heard footsteps on the stairs and rushed to the top of the staircase. She leant over the balustrade and could see her father coming up. She quickly took the plate with the sweets to her father's room and laid it down on the table.

Sutapa had realized that if her family found out that her mother had died from poison in the sweets, then Ranbir and she would be natural suspects.

As soon as Subodh entered his room, Sutapa hurried down the stairs to check on her grandparents. When she saw that they were watching television and had not yet sensed what had been going on upstairs, she went back to the first floor. She moved the curtain aside and peeped into her father's room. She saw that her father had consumed all the sweets. He was writhing on the floor, struggling to breathe. His face was contorted with pain. Sutapa felt sorry for her father, but that was not the time to let her sadness weaken her resolve. There was still a lot left to be done.

Before long, Sutapa could hear her grandmother calling out for her mother. Not hearing back from Sujata, her grandmother next called out for Subodh. She did not hear back from him either. After a while, Sutapa could hear her grandmother's footsteps on the stairs. When the old lady came upstairs, Sutapa intercepted her.

"Where are your parents? I've been shouting myself hoarse! It's almost dinner time and your mother doesn't seem to care," Lalita Mitra said, making no attempt to hide her discontent.

"I haven't seen them, Grandma," Sutapa lied.

"They must be in Baba's room. I'll check and ask Maa to go downstairs to the kitchen," she said and passed on a plate with the poisoned sweets to her. "Why don't you try these sweets? Sir has brought them. I know how much you love sitabhog!"

The old lady took the plate and smiled. She could not wait to dig into the sitabhog, her very last helping.

Having thus taken care of her grandmother, Sutapa prepared another plate and walked down the staircase. She went to the drawing room where her grandfather reclined on the couch, watching television.

"Here, have some sweets!" Sutapa smiled at her grandfather. "Sir has brought sweets for us. All of us have had them already. I brought these for you."

Manabendra Mitra looked up at his granddaughter and smiled a toothless grin. He loved the girl and had never figured out why she was treated so badly by her mother. He was usually denied the pleasure of indulging his sweet tooth as he was diabetic, but he could always trust his darling granddaughter to snitch a few for him every time the rest of the family had sweets. Today was no exception, he thought. God bless the girl!

"Always looking out for me, aren't you?" the old man said and took the plate from Sutapa's unwavering hand.

A few minutes later, there were four corpses in the house to deal with.

Sutapa went back to Ranbir to carry out the rest of the plan. The two wiped clean every surface and every utensil that they might have touched. Next, they made sure that there was no trace of the poisons anywhere in the house.

Ranbir had brought along some copper wires. The two wrapped the wires around the corpses and plugged them into sockets in the switchboards in the respective rooms. They thought that it would give an impression that all members of the family had been killed by electrocution. Ranbir tied Sutapa's hands and feet with ropes before leaving.

Sutapa was to scream and raise an alarm to alert the neighbours after about an hour. By that time, Ranbir would have reached home. When the neighbours broke in, Sutapa would tell them that a bunch of goons had come to the house to meet her father, killed everyone and ran off after tying her up.

Ranbir left the Mitra residence at around eleven in the night.

It was about a quarter past midnight when Rabin Ghosh heard muffled cries, coming from the direction of the Mitra residence. He woke up and listened intently. As the cries got louder, he woke his wife up. Someone was crying for help. As they stepped out of their house, they saw that some of the other neighbours had also come out. A few others peeped from their balconies.

Before long, a crowd gathered in front of the Mitra residence. The main door of the house was open, and when Rabin walked in, he saw Sutapa lying on the floor of the drawing room on the ground floor, her hands and feet tied. She was desperately crying for help. The girl was in a state of panic and could barely speak.

Rabin called out for the other members of the house, but there was no response. Something was fishy! Rabin immediately freed Sutapa and came out of the house. Then he called the police.

When the police arrived, Rabin entered the house with them. Nothing could prepare him for what was about to unravel before his eyes. Rabin would not forget that night for the rest of his life.

Immediately on entering the interiors of the house, they found Manabendra Mitra lying dead in his room, his hands and feet tied with copper wires connected to a socket in the switchboard. As they walked up the stairs to the first floor, a macabre spectacle awaited them. There were three more corpses, those of Subodh Mitra, his wife Sujata Mitra, and his mother Lalita Mitra in different rooms, all tied by copper wires plugged into sockets of nearby switchboards. The cupboards and steel almirahs were open. It was clear that someone had rummaged through them.

It was evident that there had been a robbery, or an attempted robbery. All the members of the family, barring the daughter of the house, had been electrocuted.

Why did the robbers choose to spare her? It was uncanny.

An FIR to the effect was lodged at the local police station.

The investigation which was started by the local police was soon handed over to the CID. The police had recovered a packet of sweets from the vicinity of the house. Upon examination, the sweets were found to have been poisoned. The police also found a bottle of Chloroform and pieces of electrical wires. These findings, supported by the post-mortem reports, contradicted the theory of robbery, which Sutapa had tried to establish.

The post-mortem findings for the four bodies appeared to be consistent, with signs of Cyanide poisoning. The larynx and trachea of the victims were congested with blood. In each of the corpses, the tongue was corroded at places. The oesophagus and stomach of each showed signs of corrosion as well.

Interrogations in the neighbourhood by the police revealed that Sutapa was in a romantic relationship with her private tutor Ranbir, which the girl's family as well as the tutor's family had resented. When the police spoke to Ranbir, there were several inconsistencies in his statement about his whereabouts on the night of the crime. Further questioning in the school where Ranbir taught revealed that he had been making enquiries about the supplier of chemicals for the school laboratory. The trail led to Dibyendu.

It was proved beyond doubt that Sutapa and Ranbir were in a relationship. The two had been seen in movie halls. Sutapa had been seen in the company of 'an older man' in the Esplanade area of Kolkata. Sutapa's mother, Sujata, had confided in some of the neighbours that her daughter had been carrying on an illicit affair with her private tutor. Ranbir's wife, Tanuja, had also informed her close acquaintances about her husband's affair. The police also looked at the attendance registers of the school where Sutapa studied, and the one where Ranbir taught. There was a striking parity in the patterns of their absences from their respective schools.

An investigation into Ranbir's finances led the police to the pawnbroker to whom Ranbir had mortgaged and later, sold golden ornaments that had been handed over to him by Sutapa. The pawnbroker had papers on which Ranbir had signed. The signatures were confirmed to be those of Ranbir.

Ranbir used to take loans regularly as he was in a state of financial duress. He needed more money than usual to entertain his girlfriend, and also for the expenses related to the sinister conspiracy that they had hatched together. These findings proved definitively that Ranbir used to receive financial help from Sutapa.

A neighbour confirmed that she had seen two guinea pigs in the Mitra residence around twenty days before the crime, and they had not been seen since around seven days before the murders. It was clear that Sutapa had tested the poisons on the poor creatures.

Further investigations led the police to the laboratory from where the guinea pigs had been purchased on the pretext of conducting science experiments. The owner of the laboratory confirmed that Ranbir had also purchased lizards in the past. These findings substantiated the fact that the murders were premeditated.

There were at least two witnesses who had seen Ranbir arrive at the Mitra residence on the evening of the crime. In fact, one of the neighbours who had been watching *Chitrahaar* on the television that evening, clearly remembered that she had seen the lights go off in the Mitra residence around forty minutes past eight and the house remained dark till around half-past nine. She had found it rather odd initially, but she shivered on realizing that perhaps that was the time when the ruthless murderers were destroying evidences and taking care of the four corpses. They did not want the neighbours to catch a glimpse, or to have someone turn up at the door.

The police concluded their investigations and arrested Sutapa, Ranbir and Dibyendu in October 1991. The most seasoned police officials in Kolkata Police found it difficult to believe that the innocent-looking fifteen-year-old girl had the gall to collude with her lover and murder her entire family.

An officer famously remarked, "Even after arresting her, we kept wondering if we had gone wrong somewhere."

However, Sutapa had more surprises in store.

Within two days of her arrest, Sutapa declared that she was willing to confess and to narrate before the police and the court, all the details of the diabolical plan that had obliterated her family. She made a confessional statement that was recorded before the sub-divisional judicial magistrate of Barrackpore.

In December 1991, the police filed chargesheets against all three under appropriate sections of the IPC for alleged murder, criminal conspiracy and destruction of evidence. Additionally, Dibyendu was booked for abetment. Following this, in January 1992, Sutapa gave an assurance of making a full and true disclosure of the circumstances relating to the murders and requested to be pardoned.

In her testimony, which practically sealed Ranbir's fate, Sutapa stated:

> *It was Ranbir who suggested some time back that my mother be poisoned. He was even willing to help me! He gave me powdered Calmpose tablets to be mixed with drinking water. When I failed to carry out the plan, Ranbir gave me water boiled with a lizard. I did not have the nerve to follow his shocking instruction. Ranbir then got in touch with Dibyendu, who used to supply chemicals for the science laboratory of the school where Ranbir taught.*
>
> *Ranbir took me along to Dibyendu's store, but I chose to wait outside while he went in. I did not know what transpired between the two. Ranbir later handed me the poisonous chemicals. He also suggested that*

the chemicals should be tested out and got me a pair of guinea pigs.

On the day of the crime, we had gone out. Ranbir kept talking about executing the plan that night and urged me to hold my nerves. I was scared. Ranbir then threatened me by saying that if I did not help him get rid of my mother that night itself, then he would leave me for good. I was madly in love with him and could not think of a life without him. So, I agreed to play along.

In the evening, Ranbir arrived at our house around half past six with sweets, and on his instructions, I poisoned the sweets with sodium cyanide. I called my mother to the first floor and made her consume a kaala jamun, and drink water mixed with magnesium chloride. She died almost instantaneously.

In the meantime, I could hear my father walking up the stairs. Ranbir asked me to keep the sweets inside my father's room, and I had no choice but to obey him.

I then went downstairs to check on my grandparents. When I returned to the first floor, I saw that my father was dying. I was upset and ran to Ranbir, asking him why he had to kill my father. I thought it was only my mother whom we had planned to kill. Ranbir explained to me that if my father found out that my mother had died after consuming a sweet laced with poison, then both of us would be in trouble. Therefore, my father had to die.

Seeing that I was beginning to lose my nerve, Ranbir told me to leave the house so that he could carry out the rest of the plan. I was feeling suffocated and obeyed him. I left the house and decided to hang around for some time.

When I returned later in the evening, I discovered that Ranbir had also killed my grandparents. I was shocked, and then heartbroken. But there was no turning back. So, I had to follow Ranbir's orders and tie up my parents and grandparents with copper wires, plugging them into sockets in switchboards. Ranbir then tied me up and instructed me to raise an alarm past midnight, because by that time, he would be back home. My lover left me alone with four dead bodies in the house!

I acted according to the plan, and the neighbours rushed to our house to free me. They called the police. Following Ranbir's instructions, I told the police that some strangers had come to meet my father in the evening, and they had left after killing all members of my family and tying me up. Also, in the days following the crime, Ranbir stayed in touch with me, and repeatedly warned me not to confess to our crime.

However, I could not handle the guilt anymore and decided to record my 'confession'.

A fast-track trial was started against Ranbir and Dibyendu. No charges were framed against Sutapa, as she had assured that she would make a full disclosure of facts as an approver. In addition to Sutapa's testimony, there were forty-five witnesses for the prosecution.

The Sessions Court at Barrackpore pronounced life sentences for both Ranbir and Dibyendu. However, the Kolkata High Court took a different stance. It was evident that Dibyendu was not present at the crime scene. He had no knowledge about either the motive or the date of the crime. Therefore, he could not be accused of abetment to the crime. As such, the conviction by the Sessions Court was set aside by the High Court, and Dibyendu was acquitted.

As for Ranbir, it was established that he had planned and executed the inhuman murder of four innocent individuals and the sole survivor of the family was his accomplice, who herself had later testified against him. The High Court upheld the judgement of the Sessions Court and death penalty was awarded to Ranbir in its verdict dated 24 September 1998.

However, the Supreme Court felt that Sutapa and Ranbir had planned to kill only Sujata. There had never been a plan to kill Sutapa's father and her grandparents. Sutapa had always been ill-treated by her mother, and the plan to murder Sujata had been due to a sense of frustration and helplessness on the part of Sutapa, which had then influenced Ranbir.

Till the time Sutapa's mother had been made to consume the poisonous sweets and she had died, there had not been 'even the remotest desire' on the part of the appellant to murder the father and the grandparents. The court ruled that Sutapa's father and her grandparents had been killed mainly out of the confusion and fright in the minds of the killers. As such, the Supreme Court of India rejected the death sentence for Ranbir and sentenced him to life imprisonment on 7 February 2000.

Ranbir spent a long time in an open-air jail in Murshidabad and earned money by conducting coaching classes. On his release, he faced acute financial crisis, and later contacted the jail authorities for assistance. The authorities of a correctional home offered him a sum of ten-thousand rupees for opening a coaching centre. The Ramakrishna Mission also donated a sum of fifteen thousand rupees to help him set up the coaching centre.

Today, the world does not know the whereabouts of the little girl who, blinded by her love for her teacher, went to the extent of killing every member of her family with the sole purpose of being with the man she loved. Love does have a way of making us do the unthinkable.

Did Sutapa find love again? Was she blessed with the peace and happiness that she always craved for? We will never know.

To Kill for Love

5 May 2008

Suraj passed an arm around Marilyn and pulled her closer, as the deep bass of the music inside The Ultimate Pub throbbed in his ears.

His eyes hovered over Marilyn's eyes, already glazed from the whiskey sours they had been drinking, her moist lips, her neck and her shoulders which were bare, but for the thin straps of her floral summer dress. Her dress revealed a hint of cleavage where his eyes lingered just a wee bit longer.

Marilyn snuggled her face against his neck, her lips slightly parted. The fire in her breath was fanning Suraj's unbridled desire. His arousal was all too evident as he planted moist kisses up and down her neck, her musky aroma turning him on. Marilyn's hand felt feverish on Suraj's thigh, and her nails dug deeper as he sank his teeth into her earlobe. They had not noticed when the waitress had appeared at the table. She cleared her throat audibly. Suraj turned around and smiled sheepishly at the waitress.

"I hope everything's alright, sir?" the waitress asked with her characteristic plastic smile.

"Oh yes, lovely cocktails!" Suraj exclaimed, as matter-of-factly as he could. Marilyn, in the meantime, had slid a few inches away from Suraj.

"Should I repeat the drinks, sir?"

Suraj looked sideways at Marilyn and without bothering to ask, he said, "Sure, whiskey sours for both of us."

As the waitress left, Suraj's eyes went to a table a few feet away. His friends were there. Nihal looked in his direction and winked. Suraj winked back and inched closer to Marilyn. She finished her drink in a long swig and looked into Suraj's eyes. Suraj passed an arm around her waist and brought his face close to hers. Marilyn closed her eyes and Suraj's lips landed on hers. He kissed her, first the upper lip, and then the lower. Their hearts fluttered in rhythm with the frenzied beats of the music as their tongues wrestled, only to disengage after a few seconds, as the waitress arrived with the next round of drinks.

Suraj stood up, heading towards the washroom. On his way, he stopped at his friends' table. He bent down and spoke into Nihal's ears, "Bro, would you mind if I use your spare room tonight?" Nihal looked up at Suraj and smiled. Suraj winked meaningfully, adding, "I can't possibly take her to Prashant's house." Prashant Bedi was Suraj's cousin, with whom Suraj shared a flat in Mumbai.

Nihal smiled and said, "Of course, bro! You don't need to ask."

Nihal had known Suraj for more than a year-and-a-half, since the time when Suraj worked in the creative team of Balaji Telefilms. Suraj now worked for Synergy, a company that produced television serials. Suraj had mentioned Marilyn Nagaraj a couple of months back and had shown her pictures to Nihal.

"Dude, she's a bombshell. Mark my words! She will make it big in Bollywood. She has already done some ads and movies down south. The camera absolutely loves her! If you know someone looking to cast a girl in a lead role, get in touch with me," Suraj had sounded excited about the new girl in his life.

He had known her since March. Apparently, Marilyn had approached him for opportunities in Mumbai and the two had got to know each other over lengthy conversations on the phone. Marilyn had finally arrived in Mumbai on 29 April. Suraj had introduced her to Nihal, and Nihal had seen them together in the coffee shop near Suraj's office, the usual hangout of the gang, every afternoon over the last few days. As he watched them kissing passionately in the pub that night, at a table away from the friends', Nihal realized that the two had got rather close in very little time. *Often, such a rushed and passionate relationship is a recipe for trouble.*

As Suraj walked towards the washroom, Marilyn fished out her mobile phone from her purse. She had deliberately silenced her phone. As she unlocked her screen, her face fell. Just as she had expected!

There were eight messages and thirteen missed calls from David, her fiancé.

Marilyn Nagaraj had very few friends and had grown up amidst rumours of impulsive affairs, none of which had lasted long. Her only steady relationship was with David Mathew, whom she had known from her school days. She always had towering ambitions of making it big in the glamour industry. After tasting success down south in a few movies and advertisements, she wanted to step into Bollywood.

Lieutenant David Mathew was an officer in the navy, based in Kochi. David had been a brilliant student, and his family was proud of him. David was polite by nature. He was known for his unconditional loyalty to those he loved and cared for, but he had a temper which was unforgiving. He could go to any lengths to seek revenge if he was ever messed with. While David was madly in love with Marilyn, his conservative parents did not approve of their relationship. David, however, was ready to go against his parents' wish for the love of his life. He had planned to marry Marilyn in the next couple of months. Like a loving and indulgent partner, he did not stand in the way of Marilyn's decision of relocating to Mumbai to try her luck in Bollywood. But, he had made it very clear that he would stay in touch with her all through the day, every single day. At times, the possessiveness of her fiancé made Marilyn feel suffocated.

Marilyn had pinned her hopes on Suraj Bedi, who she thought was her ticket to fame and fortune in Bollywood. Suraj had given her the impression that he had acquaintances in all the right places. In fact, he had promised to help her land a lead role in a mythological television serial that was being produced by one of the largest production houses of the country. Suraj, in the meantime, had fallen for the dusky dame and had not hesitated to express his feelings to Marilyn and his close friends. Even though Marilyn and Suraj started seeing each other, Marilyn maintained that she did not reciprocate Suraj's feelings. However, Suraj was confident that it was but a matter of time before Marilyn would come around.

On the night of 6 May 2008, Suraj went to meet Marilyn, and was never seen again.

❖

6 May 2008

Marilyn stepped out of the elevator along with Kishori Paranjape and the two walked towards their flats. Marilyn had received the keys of her flat in the B-wing of Dheeraj Solitaire apartment in Malad earlier in the day, and had been to the shopping mall to purchase essentials before moving in that evening. Kishori was her neighbour and lived in the flat right opposite. Marilyn had seen her a couple of times during her visits to the flat along with the agent. That evening, they had run into each other at the mall.

Marilyn entered her flat and dropped the bags on the floor. It was a warm and humid evening and she badly needed a shower before she could set up the place and cook dinner. She walked into the toilet and stepped out immediately. She had repeatedly requested the agent to get the toilet cleaned before she moved in, but he had not kept his word. She would have to call him to get it done, first thing the next morning.

Marilyn picked up fresh clothes and a towel and came out of her flat. She knocked on Kishori's door. She could hear the television inside. Kishori opened the door after a while and smiled at Marilyn.

Marilyn said, "Kishori, I'm so sorry to bother you, but the agent did not get the toilet cleaned, and I badly need a shower. I was wondering if I could use yours, unless..."

Kishori sensed Marilyn's hesitation and did not let her finish. "Oh, come on! That's not a problem at all." She stepped aside and gestured at Marilyn to walk in.

Marilyn felt rejuvenated after the shower and returned to her flat after thanking Kishori profusely.

It was around half-past ten when Suraj called.

"Marilyn, care to join me? One of my buddies has thrown a party, and he'd be more than happy to have you as a guest!

It isn't too far from Malad and I can pick you up on my way," Suraj said.

"Not tonight, Suraj. I moved in today, and there's so much to do," Marilyn replied.

"But I'm missing you, sweetheart. Can't wait to see you," Suraj sounded deflated.

"I'd have loved to come along Suraj, but you should see the mess here!" Marilyn tried to persuade him.

About twenty minutes later, the doorbell rang.

Marilyn ran to the door and opened it.

It was Suraj.

He was standing outside, with a bottle of wine and a pizza carton in his hands. He was talking on the phone which was held in the crook of his neck. "I told you Nihal, I won't be able to make it tonight. Marilyn has moved into her flat today, and I'm going to help her set up the place. It's a lot of work, yaar!" Suraj winked at Marilyn as he ended the call, even as he heard his friends complaining at the other end of the line.

Hearing voices in the corridor, Kishori opened the door of her flat.

"Hi Kishori, this is my friend Suraj," Marilyn introduced the two to each other. "And Suraj, this is my friend and my neighbour, Kishori. She's an angel!" Kishori and Suraj smiled at each other. They exchanged warm greetings as Suraj stepped in and Marilyn closed the door.

Once inside, Suraj put the wine and the pizza down on the table and hugged Marilyn tightly. "I had to see you tonight, Marilyn," Suraj whispered, as he showered kisses on her face.

"You're mad!" Marilyn punched Suraj in the chest playfully and said, "Now, let me go! The food is getting cold."

❖

Marilyn and Suraj were on a mattress in the bedroom, drinking straight from the bottle of wine which Suraj had brought along. "We must buy some glasses before you throw the house-warming party," Suraj joked.

Suraj had a meeting in Malad the next morning and had decided to stay back in Marilyn's flat for the night. "The mattress would do just fine," he had said. Now, as Suraj pulled her close and kissed her, his hands caressing her thigh over her nightdress, Marilyn wondered if Suraj really had a meeting in the morning. The wine was beginning to kick in and the gentle breeze was making its way through the open windows, fanning the desire simmering in her heart.

The buzz of the phone pulled Marilyn out of her reverie.

It was David.

Marilyn pushed Suraj away gently and took the call.

"Hi," she said.

"Hi, honey. Did you move in today? You didn't reply to my messages."

"Yes, I moved in this evening. I was too busy throughout the day. Didn't have the time to check my phone," Marilyn tried to explain.

Sitting inches away from Marilyn, Suraj could hear the conversation. "Is that your boyfriend?" he asked, in a jocular tone.

"Who's that? Are you with someone?" asked David. He had heard Suraj's voice.

Marilyn's heart skipped a beat.

"Yes, it's Suraj. He's been helping me set up the place."

"What's he doing there so late?" David sounded miffed.

"It got late, and we ordered some food," Marilyn explained. "He'll be leaving after dinner," she added.

Marilyn's phone beeped, and she looked at the battery. It was about to die.

"David, my battery is about to die. Can you call me on Suraj's phone? Take down his number," Marilyn dictated Suraj's phone number.

She ended the call and breathed out.

"Why the hell did you give him my number? He sounds like a clingy boyfriend!" Suraj did not look particularly happy about the situation.

"That way, he won't be suspicious. He'd think, if I were really up to something with you, I'd not give him your number." Marilyn winked. "See? That's how you deal with nagging boys!"

"You're wicked, you know that?" Suraj nodded his head and smiled.

Within seconds, Suraj's phone rang.

He took the call and passed his phone on to Marilyn. He could hear David speaking agitatedly at the other end of the line.

"When is he going to leave?" David shouted at Marilyn.

"I told you, David. He'll leave as soon as we're done eating," Marilyn replied sternly.

"Your friend must realize that it's very late and you live alone! What kind of a man is he?" David's rant was clearly audible. Marilyn felt embarrassed, as she looked apologetically at Suraj.

Suraj took a long swig of the wine and said, "What kind of a boyfriend are you to assume that your girl would need the company of another man?"

"What did the bastard just say? Give him the phone," David screamed at the top of his voice.

"David, calm down! You're getting this completely wrong," Marilyn said. "And please mind your language!"

"Mary, I told you to give him the fucking phone!" David was in no mood to listen.

Suraj snatched the phone and shouted into it, "Talk to me, motherfucker! What are you scared of, you insecure asshole?"

"Suraj, no!" Marilyn cried out in alarm, "Don't provoke him!"

She walked to one of the windows and stared at the darkness outside. She felt angry and vulnerable. That was what David did to her all the time. At that moment, she needed someone strong and reliable, someone who understood her. Not someone immature and judgemental like David.

Suraj ended the call. He walked up to Marilyn and hugged her from the back. "I feel sorry for you," he whispered into her ears, moving her hair aside, kissing her on the neck. "How do you manage to put up with an asshole like that?"

Marilyn turned around and buried her face in Suraj's chest. Suraj saw her shoulders shaking as she broke down. He kissed her on the head and said, "Don't cry, honey. Everything will be fine."

He stole a glance at the phone. It kept ringing continuously. "Must be the lunatic," Suraj said. He brought Marilyn back on the mattress and took her in his arms. He wiped her tears and kissed her. Marilyn kissed him back, pressing herself against his body. Suraj looked at his phone one last time. He picked up the phone and switched it off. He threw it away and went back to Marilyn.

"Is everything alright?" Ajay Pande asked David as he walked into the room which the two shared at the base in Kochi. "Where do you think you're going so late in the night?"

It was half-past eleven, and David was getting dressed. He looked upset. Ajay wondered why.

"David, what's the matter?" Ajay asked again.

"I'll have to fly to Mumbai," David finally spoke. "There's a flight at quarter to four in the morning. I've already booked a ticket."

"Are you out of your mind?" Ajay asked David, "You know the rules, don't you? You'll need to apply for leave. You can't just leave the base without informing anyone. There would be disciplinary action against you."

"I couldn't care less," David said, as he put on his shoes. He was in no mood to listen to Ajay. He stood up and left the room, slamming the door behind him.

He had to find out what his fiancée was up to in Mumbai, before it was too late.

Kundan Jha stood up from his chair at the security desk at B-wing of Dheeraj Solitaire. He stretched his arms and aching back, letting out a noisy yawn. It was half past seven in the morning. The tea stall outside the gate had opened a while back, and he badly needed a glass of tea with extra sugar. It had been his third night in a row that week, and he could not wait to get back home and crash. If only Satish turned up on time for the next shift.

Kundan looked at the gate one more time. But, instead of Satish, he saw a boy in his mid-twenties who walked in briskly. The boy appeared to be in a rush.

"Hello, sir," Kundan called out to the boy. He opened the visitors' register and said, "You need to make an entry here."

The boy did not bother to stop. "I don't have the time for this," he said as he ran towards the elevator. "I'm going to 201B. I have a relative staying there."

Before Kundan could stop him, the boy had already slipped inside the elevator.

Marilyn was woken up by the doorbell.

Suraj's naked body felt warm behind her, his arm around her bare torso. She could not remember when they had fallen asleep, after the heavy drinking and torrid sex all through the night.

The doorbell rang again.

Marilyn removed Suraj's arm gently and looked at him. Suraj was in deep sleep, snoring mildly, his mouth open and his hair dishevelled. He looked cute in his carefree sleep, Marilyn thought. She found her panties at the foot of the mattress. The flimsy nightdress was on the floor, where Suraj had thrown it casually last night. She got dressed quickly and walked towards the door in quick steps. She could tell from the repeated ringing of the bell that whoever it was at the door, was in a hurry.

"Who is it?" Marilyn asked, as she opened the door.

For a few seconds, Marilyn could not breathe. She stood rooted to the spot.

It was David!

David stepped into the flat, grabbing Marilyn by her arm and pushing her aside.

"Where is he? Where the fuck is he?" David kept repeating as he looked around, trying to locate the bedroom. When he found it, he almost ran towards it. Marilyn tried to stop him, but she already knew that it was too late.

David stood at the door for a few seconds, his barrel chest rising and falling with his heavy breathing as he glared at the man on the mattress. Suraj had woken up by that time and was trying to find his clothes. David grabbed Suraj by the hair.

Suraj knew who the man was. Marilyn had shown him David's pictures last night.

"Look, I can explain," Suraj mumbled. Not bothering to speak, David started raining blows blindly. Suraj tried to fight back, but he was no match for the navy officer who was fuming. Suraj already had his lips split open and the blood flowed freely. There was blood oozing from his broken nose and the swelling around his left eye had reduced it to a slit. David kept kicking Suraj with his boots between his naked thighs, making Suraj breathless, his face contorted in the excruciating pain. His screams reverberated in the room, even as there was a sharp crunching sound when David's knees landed on his ribs. Marilyn made futile attempts to stop David till she was flung to one corner of the room. David ran to the kitchen and returned with a knife.

"No, David, no!" Marilyn screamed, trying to get back on her feet.

David plunged the knife into Suraj's stomach even as the man cried out with the last vestiges of strength that he was left with, "Marilyn! Marilyn! Save me, please!" The first stab was so savage that Suraj's intestines spilled out. His helpless pleas were drowned in David's guttural animal cry as he kept kicking and stabbing his prey. Drenched in sweat, his eyes blood shot, the drool oozing past the corners of his lips and his face speckled with Suraj's blood, the David that was in front of her was not the man Marilyn had known all her life. It seemed as if a dangerous beast, that had been held captive inside him for years, had been set free. It was on a rampage, driven by its insatiable thirst for blood. David kept thrusting the knife in and out of Suraj's chest and abdomen, long after he was dead, every inch of his naked body soaked in blood.

"Stop it, David! He is dead. Stop it, please," Marilyn cried out, as she finally managed to get up, and tottered towards David.

David finally stopped and threw the knife away. He turned towards Marilyn and lunged at her.

"I'm...I'm sorry, David—" Marilyn whimpered, but was cut off as David slapped her across her face. The slap stung her cheeks. The roots of her teeth ached as David kept slapping her, grabbing her by her hair.

"Why did you fuck him? Why the hell did you fuck him?" David screamed, as tears kept streaming down his cheeks, "Am I not man enough for you, fucking slut?"

"No, sweetheart, no! You know how much I love you. I've been missing you so much," Marilyn tried to pacify the monster, ruffling his hair, caressing his cheeks. "Suraj was supposed to leave after dinner last night. But he stayed back and started acting funny. He came on to me, and I was too drunk..."

David grabbed Marilyn by her neck and threw her on to a mattress, next to the one on which lay Suraj's blood-soaked body. In a flash, he pulled down her panties and spread her legs. He unbuckled his belt and pushed his denim trousers and his brief down to his knees.

"Make love to me, David! I've always been yours," Marilyn whispered.

Marilyn winced and sank her teeth into her lips as David entered her and then worked up a frenzied rhythm. Marilyn felt numb with the sharp pain. David's blood-streaked face was within inches of hers. She found herself looking frequently at the corpse on the adjacent mattress, its white sheets drenched in blood, even as she started moving her hips in rhythm with David's thrusts, feeling his manhood stretch her and fill her up like never before. When he came inside her, it seemed to Marilyn that all the anger and frustration that had snowballed inside him had finally been released.

After he had come, David pulled his limp organ out. His breathing was finally restored to normal. Pulling his trousers up, he sat down on the floor and ran his fingers through his hair. As he looked around himself, the enormity of the crisis that the couple faced slowly began to sink in.

"David, we need to keep ourselves calm and work our way out of this mess," Marilyn whispered.

David nodded. He looked at the blood stains all over himself and said, "Mary, the first thing we need to do is take a shower and clean ourselves up. Then we'll need to take care of the body."

Marilyn agreed, and the two headed for the shower. Even though the toilet was not clean enough, it did not matter to

Marilyn anymore. Marilyn and David removed their clothes and got under the cold shower.

They made love once again, as the water swept the last traces of Suraj off the body of the woman he had fallen madly in love with.

Around eleven in the morning, Marilyn landed up at Hypercity Mall. There was a long list of items that she had planned to purchase to execute the plan that the couple had come up with. The items included a chopper, an air freshener and two large duffel bags.

David had ordered that Marilyn should be back in forty minutes. He had threatened that if Marilyn decided to run, then he would kill himself. Marilyn knew that David was very unstable at that moment and he was perfectly capable of doing just that. She decided not to take a chance, as the last thing she needed was another corpse in her flat. That would set the cops on her heels even if she managed to run away. Instead, she could use David's help to get rid of Suraj's body.

Marilyn got into a minor scuffle with the girl at the check-out counter over some loose change. The girl at the counter had to exercise restraint and remember all her lessons on customer sensitivity from the induction programme. She dealt patiently with the woman who was clearly under a lot of stress and kept calling her 'an idiot'. Her ordeal ended when the woman finally decided to use her debit card to pay for her purchases instead of paying by cash.

David kept talking to Marilyn on the phone all the time. Marilyn knew that David was keeping a tab on her movements, and any kind of protest would be futile.

When Marilyn walked into her flat, she found the stench of death unbearable. She saw that David had emptied two of her bags, as well as all the plastic bags from her shopping in Hypercity Mall the previous evening. David picked up Suraj's body from the mattress and dragged it along the hall to the toilet. Marilyn kept her eyes off the body all along.

"Clean the bedroom and the hall, and then help me with the packing," David said as he picked up the chopper Marilyn had bought. Then, he headed towards the toilet. "We will need a car. See if you can arrange for one," he added.

Marilyn kept looking at the trail of blood that the body had left.

As Marilyn scrubbed the blood off the floor, the sound of the chopper breaking bones reverberated in the flat. After a couple of hours, when she was done with cleaning the floors, Marilyn went to the toilet with the bags. While David kept chopping the body and piling the bloodied pieces of flesh and bones, Marilyn packed them into the plastic bags, which were finally transferred into the travel bags.

They also packed their clothes, the bedsheets and pillows, the covers of the two mattresses, all of which had been tainted by Suraj's blood in one way or the other.

Marilyn called up a friend, Karan, who was a choreographer by profession and had worked with Marilyn on some of her audition CDs. She asked him if he would be kind enough to let her use his car for a few hours. She told him her fiancé was in Mumbai and she wanted to go shopping with him in Dadar. She added that her fiancé also wanted to visit his relatives in his native town. Karan agreed, and at half-past three in the afternoon, Marilyn reached Karan's house in an auto rickshaw, along with David. David thanked Karan for his kind gesture, as the latter handed Marilyn the key to his grey Santro.

"What are friends for!" Karan hugged Marilyn and said, smiling broadly.

Marilyn drove the car and went straight to a petrol pump in Lokhandwala. David got down from the car and returned after a while, carrying two plastic cans. He filled one of the cans with five litres of petrol.

It was half-past four in the afternoon.

Satish Kumar's duty at the security desk at B-wing of Dheeraj Solitaire had started at half-past eight in the morning, like every other day. He strolled to the tea stall outside the road to buy a glass of cardamom tea. Finishing the piping hot tea as fast as he could, he started walking back towards his desk.

There was a Santro parked in front of B-wing. He had not seen the car before. He saw Marilyn and David loading bags in the boot. Satish knew that Marilyn had rented a flat in B-wing and had moved in last evening.

"Is that your car, ma'am?" Satish asked Marilyn. He would need to make a note of the registration number of the car, if the new tenant meant to use the parking lot. Marilyn smiled and said that it was a friend's car. David, in the meantime, had finished loading all the bags.

Marilyn sat on the driver's seat and started the car. David sat next to her.

"Is something bothering you?" Marilyn glanced at David and asked.

"Too many witnesses," David said. "Do you know the lady who saw us getting into the elevator?"

"She's Kishori. She lives in the flat opposite to mine. She didn't look suspicious at all, when I told her that we were going out. Relax, David!"

Marilyn stopped the car about a kilometre away from a petrol pump at Andheri East. David went to the pump, carrying a plastic can. When he asked for petrol, the owner of the pump refused. He said that his car was nearly five kilometres away and he had run out of fuel. He showed his navy badge and said that he was a senior officer from the navy and that his wife was waiting in the car. The owner of the petrol pump finally gave in and filled the plastic can with five litres of petrol.

The car now headed towards the Mumbai-Ahmedabad highway. About a kilometre from the toll plaza, Marilyn stopped the car near a shop selling *paan-beedi*, cigarettes and soft drinks. David walked up to the shop and asked the shopkeeper, Amar Yadav, if he sold cigarette lighters. Amar said that he did sell lighters, but he would have to check if he had any left. Amar went to a storeroom behind the shop and returned with a lighter. It was the last piece that he had. David paid for the lighter and got into the car.

The car now picked up speed. Marilyn drove towards Manor, about ninety kilometres to the north of Mumbai on the Mumbai-Ahmedabad highway. David, who had earlier trained at INS Shivaji at Lonavala, knew the jungles of Manor well. Daylight was fading and the sky had an orange hue. Traffic on the highway was sparse. The wind moaned in Marilyn's ears as it blew over the dry and arid fields around her. The trees near the horizon looked like blotches of ink on the sky.

It was around seven when the car took a right turn off Wada Road. There was no sign of human habitation within a radius of three kilometres from the area. The road went right through a forest. The tall trees blocked whatever was left of the dying daylight. The air inside the forest was cold, a sharp contrast with the heated asphalt of the highway. All that could be heard were the hum of the car engine and the wind rustling through the leaves. The car went past a hillock and then, turned left into a narrow track that meandered through the forest. Marilyn stopped the car there and switched off the headlights.

David pulled the bags out of the car and dropped them behind a bush. Marilyn handed him the two cans of petrol they had purchased from two different petrol pumps. David doused the bags with petrol and set them on fire, using the lighter he had purchased a while back. In no time, the flames leapt up into the sky.

David rushed back to the car and started the engine as Marilyn sat beside him. The car sped off, leaving behind clouds of dust, the cacophony of birds tearing through the ominous silence all around, and the stench of burning flesh.

There were a few more things that Marilyn and David had to take care of to cover their tracks.

David stopped the car for a few seconds on the highway on his way back and threw the plastic cans into a bush by the side of the road.

Next, as he drove into the city, David stopped the car at a bedding store. Marilyn got down from the car and went to the storekeeper, Kamlesh. She needed new covers for two mattresses. When Kamlesh wanted to note down her name and address so that he could send his boys to her residence the next morning, she insisted that they should accompany her to the flat right away to bring the mattresses to the store. Kamlesh said that she would, however, still be required to visit the store the next morning to choose the material for the covers. Thereafter, two boys from the store, Sadiq and Mehboob, accompanied the couple to Marilyn's flat and took away the two mattresses.

At around nine in the night, Marilyn called a painting contractor, Deepak Shukla, to whom she had been introduced by the real estate agent. There were blood stains on the wall, which she had not been able to remove completely. She told Deepak that she was planning to paint a part of the flat and he should meet her the very next morning.

However, Marilyn's destiny had its own designs.

Suraj's father, Kedarnath Bedi, ran a stationery shop in Kanpur. He hoped that someday, his son would return to Kanpur and take up the family business. Suraj called his mother Neelima Bedi, twice every day; around ten in the morning before he started his day and around eleven in the night, before he went to bed.

When Suraj did not call Neelima on the night of 6 May and then, on the morning of 7 May, she assumed that Suraj was busy and would call her later in the day. However, when Suraj did not call till late in the evening, his parents got worried. They made several calls to his mobile phone, but every time, they heard that his phone was switched off. When the anxious parents got in touch with Prashant, he tried to reach Suraj on his phone, but in vain. Prashant, in turn, got in touch with Nihal and his friends, but none of them had any clue about Suraj's whereabouts. They knew that Suraj had visited Marilyn the night before, and they had not heard from him through the day.

Nihal called Marilyn at about ten in the night. Marilyn told him that Suraj had left her flat at around one the previous night to attend a party at Andheri and had left his phone behind. The phone was switched off, and she had not turned it on. She had been very busy herself throughout the day, as her fiancé had come down from Kochi to meet her and she had been out with him. She added that Nihal was most welcome to come down to her flat, and she would hand Suraj's mobile phone over to him. Marilyn tried to hide her anxiety, as much as her acting skills permitted. However, Nihal had an uncanny feeling that something was amiss.

If Suraj had left his phone in Marilyn's flat last night, why had he not returned to pick it up? Why had Marilyn not called Nihal or any of Suraj's other friends and tried to get in touch with Suraj to return his phone? Why would Suraj switch his phone off if he had been planning to go to a party in Andheri last night? Why had Marilyn not turned the phone on anytime during the day?

Nihal and Prashant immediately decided that they should file a missing person's report at the Malad police station.

Nihal arrived at Dheeraj Solitaire at half past ten. When Marilyn handed Suraj's mobile phone over to Nihal, he told her that they were going to Malad police station to file a missing person's report, and since Marilyn was the last known person who had been with Suraj before he went missing, she should accompany them. Marilyn agreed. David made small talk with Nihal as Marilyn got dressed. Marilyn then left with Nihal while David stayed back.

In the police station, Marilyn issued a false statement about her activities in the past twenty-four hours. When Karan called her to check when she would be able to return the car, Marilyn informed him about Suraj's mysterious disappearance and said that she was at the Malad police station with Suraj's friends. She further informed that she would not be able to return the car before the next morning.

The next day, Marilyn and David continued to execute their plan.

When the painting contractor, Deepak, arrived at around ten in the morning with a painter, Kishori was in Marilyn's flat. As Marilyn had thought, Kishori had not suspected anything, and was her usual jovial self that morning. She left when the painters arrived.

Marilyn told Deepak that she wanted to get one of the walls of the bedroom painted first. Deepak and his painter, Saif, examined the walls.

"What are these?" Deepak narrowed his eyes and looked at a few spots on the wall. "Don't think they were here when we checked the flat before handing it over to you," he added.

Marilyn's heart skipped a beat. She clenched her fist and reminded herself to not panic. There was no way one would imagine that those were blood stains. She forced a smile and said, "I guess I should've been more cautious during the move. I must have spilled something!"

The painters smiled back and Marilyn could finally breathe. It was decided that the bedroom wall would be painted immediately.

Later that morning, Marilyn went to the bedding store to select the designs for the covers of the mattresses. This time, the storekeeper made a note of her name and address. She also paid an advance for the work, against a receipt. After that, she returned the car to Karan.

The police, in the meantime, had been carrying on their search for Suraj. When they questioned David, they found no discrepancies between his statement and Marilyn's. However, Suraj's friends and his parents, who had flown down to Mumbai from Kanpur, had their doubts about Marilyn.

On 9 May, David returned to his base in Kochi.

Little did he know that it would not be long before his 'karma' would catch up with him.

Spurred by the statements of Suraj's family and friends, the police started probing into Marilyn's movements.

When the police looked at CCTV footages from Hypercity Mall, they were intrigued by the choice of items she had bought on the morning of 7 May.

Marilyn had initially told the police in her statement that she had borrowed a Santro car from David's friend, Jayesh, for driving her fiancé around Mumbai and to visit his family in his native town. Jayesh was a naval officer based in Colaba. When Marilyn came to know that Jayesh had been out at sea at the time of the incident, she requested him to stand by her if the police interrogated him. Jayesh, however, refused to lie as his travel records would prove otherwise, and he was in no mood to jeopardize his career in the navy. Marilyn then, had no choice but to admit to the police that she had lied. She revealed Karan's name. When the police interrogated Karan, he confirmed that Marilyn had indeed borrowed his car to go for shopping with her fiancé at Dadar and to visit his relatives. The police started looking into the location records of Marilyn's mobile phone. It was revealed that she had actually been near Manor, when she claimed that she had been in Dadar.

Due to the support of Suraj's contacts, the case very quickly came under the radar of the police commissioner of Mumbai and the investigation gained momentum.

Finally, on 21 May, after hours of interrogation by the investigating officer, Marilyn broke down and confessed. She was immediately arrested. The police found out from Marilyn's call records that between 7 May and 20 May, David had called her nearly a thousand times. On 22 May, a special team went to the naval base at Kochi and brought David back to Mumbai. He was arrested too.

Immediately thereafter, Marilyn changed her stance. She offered to help the police in the investigation, and in the process, tried to put the blame entirely on David, suggesting that she had unwillingly been drawn into the feud between two men that had resulted in the murder of one by the other.

She led the police to the forests of Manor where the police found the half-burnt remains of a human skeleton. They seized the rib cage, a femur bone and the remains of the skull. The police also found a half-burnt chain of beads, a chain with a pendant of the *Gajmukh*, half burnt pieces of bags, a partially burnt bottle of deo spray, partly burnt metal buttons and coins. The police also collected samples of the soil mixed with ash.

The chain of beads and the pendant were identified by Suraj's father, his cousin, and by his close friend Nihal. The police collected blood samples of Suraj's parents, Kedarnath and Neelima, for DNA tests. Forensic experts also separated the femur bone and three teeth from the remains of the skeleton for DNA tests.

The police next visited Marilyn's flat in Dheeraj Solitaire and it turned out to be a goldmine of evidences. The forensic experts, who visited the flat along with the police, found reddish black spots of blood on the wall outside the toilet and collected scrapings of the wall as evidence. The experts detected blood stains on the lower part of a curtain in the bedroom and they cut out that portion of the curtain. They also found a faint blood spot on the inner knob of the bedroom door. Similarly, a blood spot was found on the television screen. None of these had been noticed by Marilyn when she had cleaned the house after the murder had been committed. Surprisingly, it had not occurred to the police during their earlier visits to the flat why Marilyn would repaint only one of the walls in the bedroom. They now realized that the intention had most likely been to hide the more prominent blood stains on the wall.

Marilyn also accompanied the police to the house of her friend Karan, and showed them the grey Santro car, which they had used to carry Suraj's mortal remains to Manor. The forensics team readily detected traces of blood in some of the accessories of the car. The police seized floor mats, seat covers of the rear seats, the boot mat, and two sun-protection screens of the rear windows.

On 28 May, Marilyn made a confessional statement before a magistrate where she effectively absolved herself of guilt in the murder of Suraj by craftily distorting certain details, and sealed David's fate.

Marilyn faced the interrogation without losing her nerve for a second, sticking to the narrative that she was the helpless innocent girl who had been drawn into a feud between two men that had ended with David killing Suraj. She also let on that she was being constantly threatened by the killer.

"Since when did you know Suraj?" the officer began his series of questions.

"I knew Suraj since March, but I have been meeting him purely for professional reasons daily ever since my arrival in Mumbai on 29 April," replied Marilyn.

"On the night of 6 May, you received a call from your fiancé. What exactly did the two of you discuss?"

"On the night of 6 May, I received a call from David. I informed David that Suraj was acting funny that night. David immediately asked me whether I wanted him to come to Mumbai. I dissuaded him saying that Suraj would leave after dinner."

"David, however, did not listen to you and reached Mumbai the next morning. What happened in your flat the next morning?"

"The next morning, at around half-past seven, when David arrived at my flat, Suraj had already woken up. Suraj was aware that David and I were about to get married. He knew David from the photos that I had shown him. As soon as David saw Suraj, he started raining blows on him. Suraj fought back. I could not control the two men and was a mute spectator. Before long, David stabbed Suraj with a kitchen knife. When I tried to scream, David shut my mouth, and threatened to kill me."

Marilyn paused for a few seconds and then continued with some hesitation, "He threw me on the mattress and raped me, never putting the knife down. I pleaded with David to take Suraj to a hospital, but David did not listen to me. He asked me to go into the toilet and take a shower. When I complied, David entered the toilet and raped me again."

"You then went to Hypercity Mall and made some unusual purchases! Why did you not inform the police when you had the opportunity to do so?"

"After around eleven in the morning, David instructed me to go to the shopping mall, and get him bags, a chopping knife and a room freshener. While I was away shopping, David kept talking to me on the phone. I could have run away or informed the police, but I did not, because I was scared. I also did not want to leave David alone, because I love him," Marilyn almost broke down.

"The manner in which Suraj's body was disposed of was gruesome, to say the least. What was your involvement?"

"It was David who chopped up Suraj's corpse into pieces and loaded them into the bags. He also packed in our clothes and the covers of the mattresses. It was David who suggested that we should drive to Manor. It was David who chose the spot inside a desolate forest, where the remains of Suraj were to be burnt. It was David who took the bags out of the car, doused them with petrol which he had purchased earlier from a pump at Lokhandwala, and burned them with a lighter he had bought on the way. I had to play along, as he kept threatening me all the while."

"Suraj's friend, Nihal, visited you later that night and you accompanied him to the Malad police station, where you issued a false statement. Why did you do that?"

"At half past ten in the night, Nihal called me and informed me that there had been no trace of Suraj all through the day. He came to Dheeraj Solitaire and asked me to accompany him to the police station to file a report. When David heard this, he threatened me that if I spoke the truth, then he would kill me, and then kill himself. I was scared and issued a false statement at the police station. I kept lying for the next several days, as David kept threatening me on the phone. I now realize that I made a mistake. That's why I am making this honest confession."

The noose was slowly tightening around David's neck.

Before long, he broke down under the pressure of police interrogation. He told the police that he had hidden the murder weapon inside Marilyn's flat. The police had earlier seized several knives from Marilyn's flat and had sent them for DNA tests, but all the tests had been negative. When the police took David to the flat, he went inside the toilet. There was a small door at the other end of the toilet that opened to a chamber. Inside the chamber, David opened the lid of what once used to be a water outlet, and fished out a knife with a plastic handle and a sharp, steel blade. He had hidden the kitchen knife inside the chute on the morning of the crime when Marilyn had gone to Hypercity Mall. Suraj Bedi's blood had dried on the blade. The police immediately seized the knife and handed it over to the forensics experts.

David also showed the police where he had hidden the chopper with which Suraj's body had been cut into pieces. It was found around ten feet away from where the police had earlier found the skeleton in Manor. The plastic cans were also found in the bushes by the highway, where David had dumped them that night.

In the meantime, the DNA of blood samples collected from Marilyn's flat, from Karan's car accessories, as well as from the remains of the corpse matched. There was also a match with the DNA of Suraj's parents.

This was supplemented by the statements of several key witnesses and circumstantial evidences.

David's travel from Kochi to Mumbai and his arrival at the scene of crime on the morning of 7 May were confirmed by Ajay Pande, David's roommate, who had asked David not to leave the base on the night of 6 May without applying for leave; David's air ticket from Kochi to Mumbai; and Kundan Jha, the guard on duty at the security desk of B-wing of Dheeraj Solitaire, who had seen David rush to Marilyn's flat.

Marilyn's purchases at Hypercity Mall were substantiated by the girl at the purchase counter who would never forget the woman who had humiliated and abused her on the morning of 7 May, the first time in her career, all because she did not have loose change; the proof of transaction on Marilyn's debit card and the tell-tale list of items she purchased at the store.

The couple's movements on the day of the murder were corroborated by Marilyn's friend Karan from whom she had borrowed the car; Satish Kumar, the guard on duty on the afternoon of 7 May, who had seen the couple loading heavy bags into a car; the man who worked at the petrol pump in Andheri from whom a handsome young navy officer had purchased five litres of petrol on the evening of 7 May and carried it to his car five kilometres away, where his wife was waiting for him; and Amar Yadav who had sold the last lighter in his stock to a young boy after making him wait for five minutes.

Marilyn's attempts to remove all traces of the crime from her flat were evident from the testimonies of Kamlesh, the owner of the bedding store, who remembered the woman who had visited his store on the night of 7 May, and had oddly insisted that he should send two of his boys to her house immediately to pick up two mattresses which needed new covers; Sadiq and Mehboob who had picked up the mattresses from Marilyn's flat that night; the verified records of advance payment that Kamlesh produced; and painting contractor Deepak Shukla who, along with the painter Saif, had seen dark stains on a wall of the bedroom, which had not been there a day back, and was asked to paint only that wall.

Their statements were corroborated by those of prime witnesses, Nihal and Kishori.

The police had a water-tight case. However, the court proceedings went on for three years till 2011.

In May 2011, Marilyn Nagaraj stood in the dock for three hours and denied everything she had said in her confession!

❖

4 May 2011

Appearing calm and composed throughout the hearing, Marilyn claimed that her confessional statement had been recorded under duress. She said that the police had detained her brother and sister, and had forced her to make the confession.

She claimed that Suraj Bedi had been just an acquaintance and she had never approached him for work. She had met him only once on 4 May 2008. She went on to say that on the night of the murder, she was not in the flat 201B in B-wing of Dheeraj Solitaire. Instead, she was staying with a friend. On 7 May, she had been to Inorbit Mall along with her sister to meet David, who had flown down to Mumbai to meet her. She met David around noon, and then spent the day with him. Thereafter, she went along with her brother and sister to the house of his brother's friend. In the night, she was called to Malad police station. Thereafter, the police would randomly detain her for several hours every day. From 18 May onwards, she was illegally detained by crime branch, Bandra Unit. On 28 May, the police made her sign a confessional statement under the threat of detaining her family on false charges.

David's lawyer argued in his defence and said that the prosecution had not been able to ascertain the exact time of Suraj's death. It could not be proved conclusively if Suraj had died, by the time David reached Marilyn's apartment on the morning of 7 May. David claimed that he had never visited Marilyn's flat in Dheeraj Solitaire. On the night of 6 May, when he spoke to Marilyn from his base in Kochi, he had the feeling that Marilyn was depressed. Marilyn wanted to see him and discuss the hardships that she had been facing during her stay in Mumbai. They decided that they would meet at Inorbit Mall the next day. Accordingly, David flew down to Mumbai. They met at the mall around noon on 7 May. They spent the day together. In the evening, David went to meet an uncle. He stayed at a hotel. On 8 May, he met his uncle again, and left on 9 May. David, however, could not produce the hotel bill, as he claimed that the bill was in a bag that had been seized by the police.

The hearings, initially at intervals, took place almost daily over the last eight months of the trial. The prosecution brought forty-four witnesses, and the defence, twenty.

The Chief Public Prosecutor stated that there was enough evidence to prove the charges levelled against the accused and that the prosecution did not rely solely on the statements of Marilyn, which she had changed several times. Initially when it was just a missing complaint, Marilyn claimed that Suraj had been with her the night before, till around half past one; then, in her confession, she claimed that Suraj had been with her in her flat all night and she put the blame of Suraj's murder on David; finally, in the court, she claimed that she had met Suraj only once in a party.

Arguing for a heavy sentence for David, the Chief Public Prosecutor said that given his naval background, David could have easily overpowered Suraj if he had perceived any threat from him. There was no need to kill him. Also, according to Marilyn's confessional statement, she had repeatedly asked David to take Suraj to a hospital. Why would David not do so, if his intention had not been to kill the man?

In his ruling, the judge said that it was crystal clear from the circumstantial evidences that Suraj stayed with Marilyn in her flat in Dheeraj Solitaire on the night of 6 May, and was murdered by David in the same flat on the morning of 7 May.

David was found guilty of culpable homicide not amounting to murder and of destroying evidence. He was sentenced to imprisonment of ten years for the killing, and three years for the destruction of evidence, the sentences being served concurrently, with three years of imprisonment already applied.

Marilyn was sentenced to imprisonment for three years, and with the jail term of three years already applied, she was immediately released.

The two also had to pay monetary fines. David was required to pay one lakh rupees and Marilyn, fifty thousand. The money was offered to Suraj's family.

Kedarnath Bedi was shocked by the verdict, which he felt was as good as an acquittal. "There should have been nothing less than capital punishment for those who snatched my son away from me," Kedarnath said, adding, "The verdict is very disappointing. Marilyn was the culprit. My son died because of her, so what if she did not wield the knife! Both Marilyn and David are equally responsible for the murder. Why were they given different sentences?"

Marilyn said, "I am just blank. How do you expect a convicted person to be happy?"

Her brother Robert said, "All we want to do now is leave this place as soon as possible and go back home."

David was seen deliberating with his lawyer for a very long time after the verdict, planning next steps. Shortly after the verdict, David turned against Marilyn and appealed to a higher court.

There was widespread public outrage across the nation over the verdict. Various media outlets were also critical of the court ruling. One national channel summed up the public sentiment as, "(Marilyn is) the 'Lady Macbeth of the Bedi case', who has gone an extreme length to feed her ambition, even if it means putting her jilted lover in the dock after encouraging circumstances that took the life of an innocent, and then disposing of his mortal remains and covering her tracks for days – cold, strong, unfeeling."

In May 2018, seven years after the verdict in the Suraj Bedi case, Marilyn was booked by Thane police, along with nine others, for allegedly cheating some businessmen for fifteen crores.

A Family Massacre

About forty-five kilometres from the city of Hisar in Haryana, popularly called the 'City of Steel' because of the presence of a large steel industry, is a place called Litani Mod.

Right in the middle of a farmland spread across a hundred acres in Litani Mod is a mansion, known to everyone as the Phogat Farmhouse. It is spread over an area of almost two acres. It stands there, head and shoulders above the other houses in the quaint neighbourhood – an obscene display of ill-gotten wealth, only to be remembered by history as the doomed abode of the Phogat family, which was grotesquely massacred by one of their very own, on an ominous August night, two decades back.

The grass has grown tall in the unkempt lawn in front of the house. There is a swimming pool that has long since dried up. The plaster has peeled off the walls of the house, here and there. One can easily tell that those walls have not been painted in years. The air is heavy with the acrid smell of death that has refused to dissolve in all these years.

As one walks into the house, the expensive chandeliers with their thick layers of dust, the cobwebs adorning the walls and the high ceilings, and the photographs of those who were once proud residents of the mansion, all conspire to send a chill down one's spine.

Raj Singh and his family moved into the house three years after the massacre of his brother's family. They threw out the furniture on the ground floor and set to fire the belongings of the woman who was the very embodiment of 'devil', whose greed and guile spelt doom for the entire Phogat family on that fateful night.

Sitting on a cot outside the mansion, one of the servants claims that the spirits of the dead still inhabit the house. The terror in his eyes reflects in the eyes of other villagers as well. The present occupants of the house battle against the fear lurking in the dark recesses of their hearts.

No one lives on the first floor of the house, where most of the gruesome killings took place. As one walks into a bedroom on the first floor that stays locked all the time, hiding from the world the scars of the bloodbath it witnessed, one finds on the bed a soft toy that belonged to a four-year-old boy, who did not live through the night.

This is the house that Bilu Ram Phogat built.

Bilu Ram Phogat started his life as a truck cleaner. What kept him awake night after night were not just the rumblings of a half-empty stomach, but his dreams of making it big. Even though he had not been born rich, he was determined to find his way to a life of affluence. He was certain that there had to be a shortcut to limitless wealth that would last for generations. Soon enough, that shortcut presented itself before Bilu Ram in the form of 'black oil'.

A quick learner of everything that was crooked and devious, Bilu Ram soon figured out that cheap bitumen could be used to make spurious oil that could be sold to the industrial units in Faridabad at huge profits. It did not take him long to get his hands dirty, literally. He traversed an arduous path that saw him frequently brushing with the law, but he never slowed down. Before long, he headed one of the biggest cartels in the underground industry. This black oil changed Bilu Ram's fortune. In no time, Bilu Ram Phogat rose to be one of the richest men in the state of Haryana.

As he broke every rule in the book and amassed a fortune, Bilu Ram was also getting increasingly hungry for prestige. He started off by making heavy donations to the village organizations and community welfare programs. He began to be invited as the chief guest in village functions. He proceeded to fund the election campaign of a political party, hopeful of being rewarded with a ticket for the ensuing elections. The party, however, did not fulfil Bilu Ram's wish. The community stood by him and accused the political party of betrayal. Sniffing an opportunity, Bilu Ram decided to fight the elections as an independent candidate. Riding on the wave of sympathy and goodwill, Bilu Ram ended up becoming an elected legislator to the Barwala assembly.

In the meantime, Bilu Ram had acquired nearly a hundred acres of farmland at Litani Mod, near Hisar. He erected his dream house over an area of two acres, right in the middle of the farmland. When Bilu Ram stood on the terrace of his house, the unhindered view of hundred acres of farmland surrounding him warmed the cockles of his heart. What a journey it had been to that terrace for the man who started off by cleaning trucks! The mansion was the talk of the town. It had a ramp, along which one could drive right up to the first floor. To the villagers, that piece of architectural marvel was nothing short of a wonder.

Bilu Ram's family had grown too. He had a son named Anil with his first wife Romi Devi, and two daughters – Sonal and Priya, whom everyone fondly called Pammi – with his second wife Kaveri. Anil was married to Sheetal, and they had three children – a son Romesh, and two daughters, Saloni and Shruti. Sonal was married to Rajeev Kumar.

However, this paradise could not sustain its happiness for a long time.

❖

Bilu's relationship with his second wife Kaveri had worsened over the years. Bitter fights between the two were common, which did not augur well for the children, especially because they were from different mothers. The most notorious among all the children was Sonal.

Right from her childhood, Sonal was the quintessential spoilt child of the rich dad. She was contemptuous, prone to violence even with the slightest provocation, and she lied through her teeth. Sonal went to Jindal School, one of the most reputed schools in the district, and later enrolled in a fashion designing course, but books did not interest her. Sonal spent her time smoking, drinking and splurging money in expensive hotels and restaurants. She threw her weight around where she was not welcomed, and if challenged, she did not shy away from threatening those whom she perceived to be her rivals with dire consequences.

At a very early age, her mother Kaveri had convinced Sonal that Bilu Ram loved his son Anil more than his daughters. And if Sonal did not take a stand for herself, Bilu Ram could end up handing the property over to his son. There were instances when Sonal took her mother's side and even slapped her father when her parents had a disagreement.

Sonal considered her father Bilu Ram as her principal adversary and looked upon herself as the lone soldier, having to battle for her own interests. Possibly egged on by the instinct of a fighter, Sonal signed up for taekwando and went through gruelling lessons to eventually earn a black belt.

It was during one of the taekwando tournaments that Sonal met Rajeev Kumar. The two fell in love. Bilu Ram was not particularly happy with Sonal's choice and he, along with his son Anil, did not hide their discontent. Sonal, defiant as she was, could not care less about the reservations of her family against Rajeev. She went ahead and got married.

The fissures that had begun to appear in the Phogat household got deeper with Sonal's marriage. Rajeev was not well-off. In the early days of her marriage, Sonal had no option but to ask Bilu Ram for money, and he grudgingly obliged. However, Bilu Ram put his foot down when Sonal's demands started mounting.

The rivalry among the siblings turned murkier when Sonal wanted Bilu Ram to transfer to her an agricultural land of forty-six acres surrounding the farmhouse. Bilu Ram refused, stating that Anil had been farming on that piece of land, and it could not be taken away from him under any circumstances.

The first rumbles of the dark ominous clouds that had started gathering over the ill-fated Phogat farmhouse, rang loud that night when Sonal, in a fit of rage, picked up Bilu Ram's gun and pointed it at Anil. Anil was stupefied and he stood rooted to the spot. Sonal, on the other hand, did not think twice before her fingers curled around the trigger and pulled it.

The sound of the gunshot was accompanied by the sudden cacophony of the night birds, ripping through the calm of the dark, empty fields. The servants sleeping in their quarters outside the farmhouse woke up in shock, their unbelieving eyes darting towards the farmhouse.

Anil was saved by the skin of his teeth as Sonal missed her aim. But, no one in the Phogat farmhouse realized that their countdown to doom had already started from that night.

23 August 2001

It was a lazy, sultry August afternoon. About six months had passed since Sonal had tried to kill her brother for a piece of the Phogat farmland.

Ranjeet Singh, one of the employees of Bilu Ram, had taken a break from his daily chores and was sipping on his chai along with Rajeev Kumar, who idled away most of his time in his father-in-law's farm. They were at the sawmill that stood by the side of the Phogat farmhouse. Rajeev's phone rang. It was Sonal.

Rajeev took her call and walked away to talk to her in private.

When he returned to Ranjeet, Rajeev told him that Sonal had planned to celebrate her sister Priya's birthday in the Phogat farmhouse that night. He would go and meet his wife, and then, the two of them would pick up Priya from her school. That would be quite a surprise for the birthday girl, as she had not been expecting them. Priya studied at the Jindal School at Hisar. After picking her up from the school, Sonal and Rajeev would bring her to the farmhouse, and the celebrations would begin. Ranjeet was happy. A party in the farmhouse meant that the servants and Bilu Ram's employees would also receive their share of sumptuous food and liquor. Rajeev left shortly thereafter.

Later that night, the servants saw Sonal reach the farmhouse with her sister Priya around ten. Before long, the birthday celebrations started. The sound of firecrackers, accompanied by the sounds of laughter and loud conversations, reverberated in the empty fields around the Phogat farmhouse as hours passed by.

It was close to midnight when Ranjeet was woken up from his sleep by the sound of footsteps. Someone walked past the servants' cottage towards the shed next to the fields. Ranjeet and his boys had been using the shed for a long time to store spare parts of tractors and farming equipment. Ranjeet got down from his cot and went to the window. He moved the curtain aside. What he saw surprised him beyond his wits!

The light inside the shed had been turned on and Ranjeet could see Sonal inside. *What was she doing inside the shed so late in the night?*

Ranjeet kept looking in the direction of the shed with bated breath.

After some time, Sonal came out of the shed, carrying an iron rod. Ranjeet tried to take a closer look and readily recognized the rod. It was the one they used to raise the tractor from the ground if it got stuck in the mud. Carrying that rod in her hands, Sonal walked past the cottage in the direction of the farmhouse.

The firecrackers were again set off after a while. Ranjeet realized that the celebrations for Priya's birthday would probably continue through the night. He went back to bed and fell asleep. The other servants had also retired to bed, as most of them had to wake up very early.

The next morning, around quarter to five, Ranjeet Singh was having his morning chai, sitting on a charpoy outside the servants' quarters. He stood up, alarmed, as he heard the noise of wheels screeching. He saw a Tata Sumo with Sonal on the driver's seat speeding out of the farmhouse and vanishing round the corner of the road ahead in a flash. His mouth still agape, Ranjeet was perplexed as to why Sonal had to rush out so early in the morning after the Phogats had partied till late. He wondered why none of the servants was asked to run the errand. Sonal was back, driving equally fast, in another half an hour.

Ranjeet went about his daily chores.

At about half past five, Ramphal, the milkman, turned up on his cycle. He was about to ride up the ramp, when he saw Sonal in the first-floor balcony.

"Leave the milk packets on the ground floor," she ordered Ramphal.

This deviation from routine did take Ramphal by surprise, but he decided to let it go. He nodded and left the milk packets in the ground floor balcony. As he was leaving, he saw Ranjeet and waved at him.

The school bus arrived at quarter to seven, its usual time. It waited for a few minutes, as Romesh never boarded the bus on time. Ranjeet walked up to the driver with a smile and made small talk.

"There was a party in the farmhouse till late last night, and chances are that Romesh would be late," he said. The driver looked irritated. To irk him further, Ranjeet added, "Romesh may still be asleep. His parents may have decided not to send him to school."

The driver looked at his watch impatiently and then blew the horn a couple of times. That usually brought the boy out of the house, running towards the bus with his mother in tow, stuffing the tiffin box inside his bag. None of that happened today.

"I cannot wait any longer," the driver said decisively. He still had to pick a few more children and make it to the school on time. The bus left, blowing a cloud of dust and smoke behind it.

Ranjeet looked at his watch one more time and called for Rohtas, one of the servants who was working in the lawn.

"Rohtas, go in and check if Romesh is ready for school. I will then drop him to school on my motorbike," said Ranjeet. He had dropped Romesh to school on several occasions in the past.

Rohtas nodded and walked up the ramp to the first floor of the farmhouse. In a few minutes, Ranjeet heard him screaming. He lost no time and sprinted up the ramp. What he saw there left him breathless.

Sonal was lying on the porch, her face contorted and her mouth frothing. She was trying to say something, but she was barely audible. Ranjeet sat down next to her on a knee. She grasped his hand and stammered, "Save me... save me, please... call Rajeev..."

Ranjeet nodded and gestured at Rohtas to stay there, right next to Sonal. He headed towards the rooms. He had to wake everyone up immediately.

Ranjeet knocked on the door to Anil's bedroom. There was no response. He called for Anil and knocked a few more times. Sensing that something was wrong, he pushed the door open and walked in. There was no trace of Anil in the room. Instead, there was his wife Sheetal, lying dead on the bed in a pool of blood, her hands and feet tied, and her mouth gagged. The lifeless bodies of her children, Romesh and Saloni, lay next to her. The three were barely distinguishable with their heads smashed grotesquely and their faces smeared with red-black blood. Ranjeet reached for the wall to support himself as the macabre scene in front of his eyes made his knees shake.

In a trance, Ranjeet walked from one room to another on the first floor. He found Anil bludgeoned to death in one, his sister Priya whose birthday the family had celebrated till late last night, in another. Ranjeet had never seen so much blood in all his life. He came out into the porch and retched a few times. He then started walking wearily up the stairs to the second floor.

By this time every day, Bilu Ram would be up, going out for his walk. Ranjeet had not seen him since morning and had assumed that Bilu Ram had been sleeping late after the party last night.

The door to Bilu Ram's bedroom was open, which was unusual. As Ranjeet walked towards Bilu Ram's bedroom, his heart pounded against his ribs. When he went closer, Ranjeet could see inside. Bilu Ram was sprawled on his bed, both his legs hanging past the edge. Ranjeet stood at the door and closed his eyes instinctively. The bedsheets, Bilu Ram's clothes and his face were drenched in blood. And, his head had been gruesomely clubbed. Ranjeet could not bear the shock anymore.

He sat down on his haunches. He had no strength left. But, a voice inside him reminded him that, he had still to check on Bilu Ram's wife, Kaveri, who slept on the top floor. Ranjeet, by now, was almost certain what to expect as he climbed up the last flight of stairs. Sure enough, Kaveri had met the same fate. Finally, Ranjeet's tears broke through the last vestiges of his restraint when he saw the blood-soaked body of Shruti, Anil's younger daughter, barely three months old, still clinging to the lifeless body of her grandmother. Her head was smashed to pulp. Ranjeet's guttural cry echoed in the house, which had turned into the playground of death overnight, with eight corpses spread across its rooms.

Ranjeet stood up. He had to save the only one whom the monster seemed to have spared – Sonal. He ran down to the first-floor porch. Sonal's eyes were closed and it did not look like there was a lot of life left in her. Ranjeet would have to call the police and an ambulance right away.

He ran to Sonal's room to make the phone calls. His eyes went to her bed. There was an iron rod lying there.

That was the same iron rod they used to lift tractors stuck in the mud. That was the same rod which Ranjeet had seen Sonal pick up from the shed and carry back with her to the house last night. There were patches of blood all over that rod!

As Ranjeet looked closely, he could see a piece of paper next to the rod.

With trembling hands, Ranjeet picked up the paper.

It was a suicide note!

Ranjeet ran back to the porch. He instructed Rohtas to get the servants together and take Sonal to the hospital. He himself started running towards the Uklana police station.

The nation was taken by storm!

The massacre of the Phogat family at Hisar was suddenly what everyone was talking about. The chief minister of the state rushed to the spot. The opposition alleged complete deterioration of the law and order machinery. Reporters had a field day. Conspiracy theorists went overdrive as they got busy outdoing one another.

Ranjeet had handed over the suicide note to the Sub Inspector (SI) who was in charge at the Uklana police station.

He had also narrated to him what he had seen and heard in the farmhouse since the night of the party. The SI had duly filed an FIR on the basis of the contents of the suicide note and the sequence of events as reported by Ranjeet. The police reached the scene of crime within ten minutes of lodging the FIR.

The Superintendent of Police told the media that iron rods had been used to kill Bilu Ram Phogat, his wife Kaveri, daughter Priya, son Anil and his wife Sheetal and their three children – Romesh, Saloni and Shruti.

The initial statement of the police was, "Preliminary investigations point to a family feud. But we are exploring all angles. Another of Bilu Ram's daughters, Sonal, who was rushed to hospital by the villagers, is in a critical condition. She holds the key to the killings. There was a party in the house last night and we are gathering information about the invitees."

A district official, who had been camping at the crime scene said, "There could be several killers. They evidently came with the aim to eliminate Bilu Ram's family. Only a thorough investigation will throw more light on the incident. The only survivor of the attack, Sonal, who is battling for life, is our clue to the gruesome killings." He also said that, by taking Sonal to a hospital, the villagers had helped save the life of the key witness.

The police took note of the fact that while all the members of the house had been clubbed to death, it was only Sheetal who seemed to have put up a resistance, and had her hands and feet tied, and her mouth gagged. *Were the other members of the family unconscious when they were clubbed to death and that was why they had not put up a fight?*

In the meantime, Sonal, who had tried to commit suicide by consuming an insecticide, was being treated at the Janta Hospital at Barwala, around thirty kilometres from Hisar.

The police started their investigation by questioning the servants and searching every nook and cranny of the Phogat farmhouse and the adjoining land.

The manager and the servants informed the police that they had seen Sonal arrive at the farmhouse on the night of the massacre, along with her sister Priya, whom she had picked up from her hostel at Hisar. The sisters had arrived at the farmhouse to celebrate Priya's birthday. The celebrations had gone on till very late in the night. The servants had heard firecrackers.

Ranjeet Singh mentioned that he had seen Sonal in the shed adjoining the fields late in the night. Sonal had picked up an iron rod. She had been seen walking in the direction of the farmhouse, where the eight corpses were discovered the next morning, all of them clubbed to death. The servants had earlier seen Sonal drive away in a Tata Sumo towards Surewala Chowk at around quarter to five in the morning, only to return to the farmhouse around half an hour later. She must have consumed the insecticide thereafter.

None of the servants, however, had heard cries for help in the night. The police found that rather odd. The observation added more credence to the suspicion that the members of the Phogat family, barring probably Sheetal who had to be tied and gagged, had been asleep or unconscious when they had been killed. To further probe the angle, the police started examining leftovers of the food that the Phogats had consumed in the night.

The police did not have to try too hard!

The police found a number of *thalis*, where traces of opium were found in the *kheer*, which the family had consumed after dinner. One of those, in fact, had two hundred and fifty grams of opium!

In the meantime, the case took an interesting turn when Sonal made a judicial confession before a magistrate.

The sanctity of the statement, however, later came into scrutiny as prosecution could not establish that prescribed protocol had been followed during the process of recording Sonal's statement at the Barwala hospital. It could not be proven that Sonal had given the statement voluntarily, both in terms of the requisite number of witnesses being present at the time of recording of the statement, as well as the availability of definitive documentation.

In fact, during proceedings in court also, Sonal denied having made the statement voluntarily. She claimed that she had been picked up by the police from Faridabad on 24 August and had been brought to Hisar, where she had been kept in illegal custody and tortured. She also said that the police had threatened her to make a statement that suited their narrative or else her only son would be killed. Thereafter, Sonal claimed, the police had forcibly obtained her signature on blank sheets of paper and submitted a false statement, claiming it to be Sonal's.

Now, let us come back to the statement that Sonal recorded before a Judicial Magistrate inside Janta Hospital at Barwala.

In that statement, Sonal went on to confess that she had murdered her family members. She said:

> *"My step-brother Anil was not on good terms with me and my husband Rajeev. My father, in connivance with him, conspired to break my marriage and dispossess us from the property. My mother invited us yesterday for my sister Priya's birthday. My husband came with me up to Hisar and returned after dropping me there. Anil, who did not join the party in the evening, uttered harsh words later. I was hurt and used the rod to kill all of them!"*

So, what, according to Sonal, exactly happened on that fateful day?

According to Sonal's judicial confession, she had been returning from her in-laws' house in Saharanpur to Litani along with her husband Rajeev, as her mother had invited them for her sister Priya's birthday. On the way, they picked up Priya from her school in Hisar. As the three were headed towards the Phogat farmhouse, there was an argument in the car between Sonal and her husband Rajeev. Rajeev got out of the car and went back to Hisar, leaving Sonal with Priya.

Later that night, Sonal was humiliated by her step-brother Anil, and in a fit of rage, she killed everyone in her family, one by one, with an iron rod. She felt that it was her own father, the head of the family, who did not love her. Being a taekwando expert, she knew exactly where to hit to kill someone. After killing everyone, she consumed poison to end her own life.

In addition to the judicial confession made by Sonal to the magistrate in the hospital, there were two other evidences against her.

The first was her suicide note, which Sonal had addressed to her husband Rajeev. In the very first line of that suicide note, she had confessed to having killed her entire family of eight, including three young children in a shockingly inhuman act. She had further mentioned that she was going to end her own life as well.

In the same letter, Sonal had admitted to writing it immediately after murdering her family. The police validated Sonal's statement with the fact that Ranjeet Singh himself had picked that letter up from Sonal's bed before he left for the police station that morning. Handwriting experts confirmed beyond any doubt that the letter had indeed been written by Sonal.

The second evidence against Sonal were the blood stains on her clothes. Examination of blood groups of the samples collected from Sonal's clothes matched with those of Anil and Romesh.

The medical evidences also stacked up against Sonal.

The autopsy conducted on the dead bodies of the eight members of the Phogat family confirmed that the injuries found on the bodies of the deceased were ante-mortem in nature which were sufficient to cause death. Those injuries could be caused by a blunt object like an iron rod. The police tallied this observation with the testimony of Ranjeet Singh who had mentioned seeing Sonal pick up an iron rod from the shed and carrying it to the farmhouse late in the night of the crime. The blood-stained iron rod had also been recovered from Sonal's bed at the place of occurrence.

However, two questions still remained.

First, why did Sonal drive to Surewala Chowk at quarter to five on the morning of the crime?

Second, did Sonal have an accomplice?

The police considered the fact that Sheetal had been found dead with her mouth gagged, her hands and feet tied. That was clearly indicative of the fact that while the other members of the family had fallen asleep or lost their senses from the effect of the opium found in the kheer that had been served at dinner, Sheetal had been awake and in her senses as she had managed to put up a resistance. Therefore, to overpower her, the killer gagged her mouth and her hands and feet were tied.

Now, by no stretch of imagination could it be perceived that the tying of her mouth, hands and feet could be accomplished by only one person. It would certainly not have been possible for Sonal alone. Therefore, there was only one answer to both the open questions.

Sonal had an accomplice in the Phogat farmhouse that night, who helped her carry out the murders. She drove her accomplice away from the scene of crime in her Tata Sumo early next morning.

The police started their investigation at Surewala Chowk.

In her judicial confession, Sonal had mentioned that she had left the place of occurrence on the morning of 24 August on a personal errand, returning to the Phogat farmhouse after about half an hour. This had been corroborated by the servants as well. The police found out that a Head Constable by the name of Dharam Singh had been on patrolling duty at Surewala Chowk from 2 to 6 in the morning on the same day. Dharam Singh confirmed that he had seen Sonal around 5 a.m., driving a Tata Sumo at high speed from the direction of Barwala.

On the face of it, there was no reason for Sonal to leave the Phogat farmhouse in the morning when she had already decided to end her life by taking poison, unless she was driving someone away from the crime scene.

The police started talking to the bus conductors in the nearby bus stop, and before long, they got lucky.

The conductor of a bus plying on the Hisar–Yamuna Nagar route recognized Sonal's husband, Rajeev Kumar. He remembered that Rajeev, wearing trousers and a bush shirt and carrying a bag, had got off from a Tata Sumo that had come from the direction of Barwala, and had boarded his bus. He had bought a ticket for Kaithal and had alighted from the bus there. The bus conductor later identified Rajeev in court.

As the police made enquiries at Kaithal, Brajesh Kumar, a taxi driver also recognized Rajeev. On the day of the crime, when he was at the taxi stand at Kaithal, Rajeev hired his taxi around half past seven for going to Panipat. The taxi driver confirmed that Rajeev was carrying a bag on his shoulder. On the way, Rajeev got down from the taxi at Jaidev STD booth at Kaithal, made a call, boarded the taxi again, and was dropped by the driver at Panipat.

The police started connecting the dots. Their next stop was Jaidev STD booth at Kaithal.

The owner confirmed that Rajeev had made an STD call from his booth on the morning of 24 August. He checked his records, and it turned out that Rajeev had called a number at Saharanpur. The owner of the booth also identified Rajeev in court.

Rajeev had indeed called a number in Saharanpur from the STD booth. It was verified by the telephone exchange at Kaithal on the basis of the list of outgoing telephone calls made from the STD booth, as well as the telephone exchange at Saharanpur where it was found that the number which Rajeev had called from the booth belonged to his residence, registered in his own name.

The police now wanted to understand how Rajeev had got into the farmhouse the night before.

Sonal, in her judicial confession had stated that she, along with Rajeev, had gone to the Jindal School to pick up Priya on their way to the Phogat farmhouse to celebrate Priya's birthday. Sonal further stated that Rajeev had an altercation with her in the car, presumably after Priya had informed Rajeev of an affair that Sonal had been having outside her marriage. According to Sonal's statement, Rajeev became very angry, got down from the vehicle at Hisar and went away. Based on the findings about Rajeev's movements the next morning, the police now understood that the whole story about Rajeev's leaving Sonal on the way to Litani after the altercation was part of the plan that had been hatched by Sonal and Rajeev to mislead the investigators.

The police went back to Sonal's statement, and the following part of her statement caught their attention:

> *At about 9 p.m. he [Rajeev] alighted from the vehicle at Hisar and started saying that I should go home alone. I waited for five to ten minutes, hoping that he would come back, but he did not turn up. After that I, along with my sister, went to our house at Phogat farmhouse*

> *kothi at Litani Mod. We reached the kothi at about 10 p.m. On the way, we purchased six pastries from the cake shop at Hisar.*

The police zeroed in on the cake shop. They questioned Paramjeet Singh, who owned the fast food and bakery shop at Hisar. In his statement, Paramjeet said that Sonal had been accompanied by another girl, and a man whom the girl called *'Jijaji'*, proving beyond doubt that contrary to Sonal's statement, Rajeev had not abandoned the sisters at Hisar after an argument.

The fact was further corroborated by the statement of another witness by the name of Ishwar Singh, who said that he had seen Sonal, along with her sister and another man, purchasing fruits at Barwala, close to the farmhouse. Ishwar Singh later identified Rajeev in court.

Rajeev initially took the stand that he was being falsely implicated. He insisted that the massacre was carried out either by those who had taken loans from Bilu Ram, or by Bilu Ram's employees who had embezzled his money. However, his resistance was short-lived.

He broke down during interrogation and disclosed that he had entered and left the Phogat farmhouse, hiding in the middle seats of the vehicles on the two occasions. After the massacre, he had put the blood-stained clothes of the couple in a bag. He had then, carried the bag to the fields near Bhainswal village and burnt it, along with the clothes inside. The police went to the location Rajeev had mentioned and recovered the ash from the burning of the clothes, a few items of clothing soaked in blood which had not burnt completely, as well as a zipper and two buttons of the bag that Rajeev had been carrying that morning.

The fact that Rajeev had been carrying a bag had also been corroborated by the bus conductor, the taxi driver and the owner of the STD booth. Forensic examination of the clothes which had not burnt fully revealed traces of blood of all eight members of the family.

Rajeev was also administered a polygraph test, during which Rajeev gave graphic descriptions of the murders. He said that the murders had started from eleven in the night and went on till four in the morning. Rajeev was initially hesitant to carry out the evil plan, but Sonal had egged him on by saying that there would never be a better opportunity.

Rajeev revealed during the polygraph test that they had first planned to use a pistol to kill the family members while the firecrackers were being burst in the party. However, they had to abandon the plan when Kaveri asked them to stop bursting the firecrackers as her husband, Bilu Ram, had gone to sleep. It was then that Sonal and Rajeev planned to use an iron rod to club everyone to death, one by one. Being taekwando experts, they knew exactly where to hit to kill someone. Sonal went to the shed and picked up the iron rod. The family had already consumed the *kheer* laced with opium.

Firstly, they went to the second floor and beat Bilu Ram to death, while he was fast asleep. They then, proceeded to the top floor, where Kaveri had already gone to sleep with Shruti. They beat both of them to death.

Then, they came downstairs. They found Anil, Sheetal and Priya having a chat. While Anil and Priya appeared drowsy, Sheetal was wide awake.

The couple told Priya that they were planning to get her admitted to a taekwando course and wanted to have a discussion with her. They took her away to a room. Once inside the room, her senses already numbed by the opium, Priya had her head smashed even before she could react. There was a loud sound, and when Anil called out to check if everything was alright, they told him that a suitcase had fallen.

The couple then told Anil that they wanted to discuss property matters with him in private in another room. Sheetal took the hint and went away to the bedroom where her children Romesh and Saloni were already asleep.

The opium was beginning to kick in and Anil wanted to have the discussion the next day. However, the couple said that they would have to leave the next morning, and insisted on having the discussion that night itself. Anil stood up gingerly and tottered with them to an adjoining room. Sonal struck quickly and cracked Anil's skull in one fatal blow.

The couple finally entered Anil's bedroom. When they went for the kids, Sheetal tried to resist. However, she was soon overpowered. The couple managed to gag her and tied her hands and feet. They then killed the children, Romesh and Saloni, and then smashed Sheetal's head.

Although Sonal tried to own up the crime alone by driving Rajeev away from the scene of crime, and later writing a suicide note addressed to him, the prosecution managed to build a strong case against Rajeev based on circumstantial evidences, the results of Rajeev's polygraph test, statements by everyone who had seen him fleeing the crime scene the next morning, and the discoveries made by the police at his instance.

The case was filed and Sonal, Rajeev as well as eight members of Rajeev's family were tried. On 31 May 2004, the Hisar district and sessions judge awarded death penalty to Sonal and Rajeev based on circumstantial evidences as well as the testimony of a total of sixty-six witnesses. The motive behind the murders was ascertained to be a dispute between Sonal and her stepbrother, Anil over the property of Bilu Ram Phogat. Rajeev's relatives, including his parents and his brother, were acquitted of all charges.

The couple subsequently filed an appeal in Punjab and Haryana High Court, and the sentence was reduced to life imprisonment on 12 April 2005.

Thereafter, Bilu Ram's brother, Raj Singh Phogat and the State Government filed an appeal in Supreme Court for the reinstatement of the death sentence. In a landmark verdict, the Supreme Court, reinstating the death sentence on 15 February 2007, said that, "both the accused persons were not possessed of the basic humanness, and completely lack the psyche and mindset which can be amenable for any reformation."

The court took note of the fact that the accused not only ended the lives of her stepbrother and his whole family, but did not spare three tiny tots, her own parents and her sister in a diabolic manner, just to prevent her father from handing over the property to her stepbrother. "The fact that the murders in question were committed in such a diabolic manner while some of the victims were sleeping, without any provocation whatsoever from the victims' side, indicates the cold-blooded and premeditated approach of the accused to cause death of the victims," the bench said.

Terming the manner of the killing of the helpless victims as 'brutal, grotesque and revolting', the court said it "is indicating of the fact that the act was diabolic of most superlative degree in conception and cruel in execution". The bench further said, "If this act is not revolting or dastardly, it is beyond comprehension as to what other act can be so."

Initially, the date of hanging was fixed for 26 November 2007, but the couple filed a mercy petition with the President of India. Their mercy petition had earlier been rejected by the Governor of Haryana in October 2007. Sonal's plea was forwarded to the Union Home Ministry for its comments. In his recommendation to the President, the then Home Minister said that, even though Sonal was a woman, considering the nature of her crime, she did not deserve sympathy. There were no extenuating factors or mitigating grounds for the then President of India to exercise her discretion for grant of clemency. Therefore, the mercy petition, the Home Minister suggested, should be rejected, paving the way for Sonal and her husband to be hanged.

Throughout the process, the couple, who had a seven-year-old child, stayed in the central jail. Even after being arrested and sentenced to death, Sonal threatened lawyers and jail officials and bullied her inmates. She even tried to escape from custody.

The petition went unresolved by the then President of India and was finally rejected by her successor on 4 April 2013, clearing the way for what would be *the first hanging of a woman in India*. The hangings were scheduled for the same month, but on the night of 6 April, the Supreme Court stayed the executions for two weeks.

In the meantime, a civil rights group by the name of People's Union for Democratic Rights (PUDR) filed a petition, requesting the life sentences for the couple be reverted to life imprisonment. They cited delays in the disposal of the mercy plea as grounds for clemency, which the Supreme Court accepted in January 2014, citing the time Sonal and Rajeev had spent in custody since their arrests in 2001 – twelve years three months until December 2013 besides delays in disposal of their mercy petitions, and in the arrival of the information about the rejection of the petitions.

❖

In May 2018, Rajeev was released on a fourteen-day parole from the Kurukshetra jail. He did not report back after the expiry of his parole.

In October 2018, Sonal tried to hang herself at the Kurukshetra jail using her saree, as reported by the jail superintendent. Prompted by this incident, as well as several complaints against her made by jail staff and other inmates, she was removed to a prison in Karnal.

The attorney in Hisar, who was the public prosecutor in the case and was tasked with proving the guilt of Sonal, still looks at the photographs from the crime scene.

They show the bloodied bodies of Sonal's family members, who had been bludgeoned to death. "*Why would a woman do this? Why would a daughter do this?*" he asks, as he recalls the case which was among the earliest examples in India of how lust and greed can defy all notions of motherly love and compassion that the society generally associates with women.

The Devil has a Pretty Face

Raj rolled off Nidhi and lit a cigarette. They were still panting from the throes of orgasm.

Nidhi pulled the sheet to cover herself and moved a few strands of her hair off her sweat-slicked face. Raj turned to look at her. His girlfriend glowed in the aftermath of their passionate lovemaking. He had never seen a woman more beautiful than her. He kissed her on the lips and then, on her bare shoulders, nuzzling his face in her neck. Nidhi ran her fingers absent-mindedly through Raj's hair.

The frenzy of their lovemaking now slowly ebbing, Nidhi was acutely conscious of her surroundings. She could hear the busy traffic on the road below. They were inside a dingy room in a cheap lodge, which Raj had hired for two hours. The air inside the room smelt of cigarette smoke and the bleach from the toilet. The tubelight flickered and the colours had faded from the dirty curtains that hung over the windows. The wall facing the bed had a wallpaper of a sunset, and was torn in places. The walls were so thin that Nidhi could hear the bed creaking and a woman groaning loudly in the next room as she got fucked. She could be a hooker, or someone like her, spending a couple of hours with a cash-strapped lover.

Nidhi realized that they must have also been heard in the rooms on both sides, as Raj had moved in and out of her a few minutes back, like a man possessed, grunting hoarsely. She looked at the sheet that covered her naked body. It was dirty, grimy and had stains here and there. The sheet on which they were lying was also filled with stains.

Raj had been caressing her bare body, and he now sat up. He grabbed a handful of peanuts from the plate and took a swig of the cheap whiskey he had ordered, getting ready for another round of sex before their time was up. He made a face as the whiskey burnt his throat. He threw away the cigarette stub and turned towards Nidhi, ready to mount her again. Nidhi looked away and gestured at him with her hand to stay away.

"Hey, what's wrong?" Raj looked surprised.

Nidhi looked at him and said, "Raj, is this how it's going to be?"

"What do you mean?" Raj sat up straight.

"Are we always going to be like this? Hire a room in a cheap lodge by the hour, drink cheap whiskey with peanuts, fuck on a creaking bed and go back to our own places?"

"Of course not, *jaan*," Raj was still not sure where this was going. He said, "You know how much I love you. We will get married, make a beautiful home, and have babies..."

Nidhi interrupted his daydream.

"For that, we'll need money, Raj. A lot of money," Nidhi sat up. Raj looked away. He knew that his odd jobs would not let him make the kind of money that Nidhi had in mind. Nidhi herself worked in a beauty parlour at a meagre salary and took up part-time marketing and telecalling jobs on the side. Neither of them was able to save anything for the future.

Nidhi took Raj's face in her palms and kissed him on the lips. "You know that I love you, don't you?" she asked. Raj nodded. "But we do not deserve this life. I want to live life king-size. Why can't we stay in a bungalow? Why can't we drive around the city in a big car? Why can't we holiday abroad? You know Raj, every time I look at Mridula ma'am, I think, why can't I be like her?"

Raj smiled dryly. Nidhi would always cite the example of Mridula ma'am whenever she talked about their future.

Beautiful and ambitious, twenty-three-year-old Nidhi Sharma worked as a beautician in Indore. Nidhi made heads turn wherever she went and she was conscious of the effect she had on men of all ages. The daughter of a taxi driver, Nidhi had studied till tenth standard. She believed that her looks and charming demeanour would be her gate-pass to a life of affluence and luxury with her twenty-four-year-old lover, Raj Malhotra. She had been with other men before Raj, but there was something about him that had got her hooked. Although she was aware of the fact that Raj was not exactly virtue personified. He had been rounded up by the police on a few occasions for petty crimes. Destiny, however, had other plans for Nidhi Sharma, who became the first woman to be sentenced to death by the Madhya Pradesh High Court. This is her story.

Nidhi had seen forty-two-year-old Mridula Deshmukh at the beauty parlour where she worked. She knew that Mridula's husband, Niranjan, was an officer in Bank of India, who lived in Pune. Mridula lived with her twenty-one-year-old daughter Anushka and seventy-year-old mother Rukmini in a large house in Sri Nagar Colony.

In June, 2011 Nidhi ran into Mridula once again.

On that day, Nidhi was working as a salesgirl for beauty products at the Orbit Mall. When she saw Mridula, she walked up to her and struck a conversation. She could not take her eyes off Mridula's gold jewellery. She wondered how much those ornaments would be worth. Her unbridled desire for easy money and a luxurious life with her lover raised its ugly head deep inside her.

"I didn't know that you also sell beauty products," said Mridula.

"Ma'am, I work part-time as a marketing agent for the company," said Nidhi, a charming smile plastered on her lips.

"That's very impressive, Nidhi," Mridula was genuinely impressed. "You see, Nidhi, I work for a cosmetics company. We follow a network system for selling. It is called Multi-Level Marketing, where one seller can hire another seller, thereby growing the sales network."

Nidhi was listening with wide-eyed wonder and the wheels had already been set in motion inside her brain. She had to find a way of getting close to Mridula ma'am.

"Ma'am, with my experience in the marketing of beauty products, do you think I can work for you?" she asked.

Mridula thought for a while and said, "Why not! We can discuss. I am in a rush right now, but we should discuss this. Why don't you give me a call some time and we can fix up an appointment?"

The two exchanged phone numbers.

"Ma'am, I'll call you in a day or two," Nidhi said.

She walked with Mridula to the parking lot of Orbit Mall. She kept looking at Mridula's large, chauffeur-driven car as she was driven off.

That evening, Nidhi and Raj were inside a room in the run-down lodge.

They had just made wild, animal love and were catching their breath. Nidhi was excited about something. She was drinking the cheap whiskey straight from the bottle. Her torso was barely covered by the sheet and her hair cascaded down her shoulders. Raj could not wait to jump on her one more time, but realized that his scheming girlfriend was surely on to something.

"Honey! I have a plan," Nidhi finally kept the bottle of whiskey down on the nightstand with a thud and said to Raj.

"A plan? What kind of plan?" Raj realized that they were not having sex anytime soon again that evening.

"I met Mridula ma'am in the mall today," Nidhi's voice reduced to a hiss. "You should have seen the gold ornaments the bitch was wearing, yaar!" Nidhi's eyes had a glazed look.

Raj kept listening.

"All those ornaments could be mine!" Nidhi said.

"What do you mean?" Raj wondered if Nidhi was drunk.

"Give me a smoke," Nidhi demanded, as she picked up the bottle and took a generous gulp of the whiskey.

Raj lighted two cigarettes and passed one on to Nidhi.

"We're going to loot her house!" Nidhi said, as she took a long drag and blew out.

"Are you out of your mind?" Raj could not believe what he had just heard.

"She lives alone with a daughter and an old mother. It would be easy!" Nidhi winked at Raj.

"And how do you think we are going to break in?"

"We don't need to break in, Raj. She's willing to offer me a job. I already have her phone number. All I need to do is call her up and fix an appointment in her house. I'll get in first and engage her in conversation. When the time is right,

I'll call you up. We'll carry arms. I am sure it won't take much to overpower them. In the worst scenario, we might just have to kill them. We'll run away with the money and jewellery." Nidhi made it sound very simple as she almost emptied what was left of the bottle.

Raj stood up and started pacing up and down the room, taking quick drags of his cigarette. The plan Nidhi had hatched did not sound impossible, after all. It would not be too difficult for him to get hold of arms. But there was something else that was bothering him.

He stopped and turned towards Nidhi.

"Do you think the two of us would be able to take care of all three of them? Even if one of them manages to slip out, or make a phone call, we would be in trouble."

Nidhi ran her fingers through her dishevelled hair and thought for some time. Then, she looked up at Raj and said, "You are right. Let's get someone we can trust. Know anyone?"

"Let me talk to Manish," Raj did not have to think too long. He was absolutely sure about the one man he could trust blindly.

"I can't wait to do this," Nidhi said. "How quickly can you make the arrangements?"

"I'll talk to Manish tomorrow," said Raj.

"Let's plan for the 19th of June!" Nidhi announced. Her eyes had a sinister shine in them. She removed the sheet and stretched her arms, inviting Raj back on top of her bare body.

That was how the thirty-two-year-old Manish Rathore became the chosen one to join Nidhi and Raj in their heinous act that would soon shock the entire nation.

❖

Munni Badnaam Hui

Darling Tere Liye…

The music blared from two run-down speakers which were held by wooden brackets on opposite walls near the counter. The chartbuster from Salman Khan's movie from last year was still a favourite in watering holes across the country.

As Raj stepped in, he was greeted by his gang of boys, who had assembled at their regular table at the far corner of the bar. One of them gestured to the waiter to bring more beer to the table.

In the dim red light of the bar, its air thick with cigarette smoke, Raj's eyes searched for Manish in the crowd. He finally saw him, reclining against the wall, his eyes closed. He was drinking straight from the bottle. Manish was older than the rest of the boys and usually appeared somewhat aloof. The boys loved him as he had fascinating stories to share from his life in the dark lanes of Indore. He was their go-to person whenever they needed arms or drugs. Manish had connections in the right places.

"Hello Manish bhai," Raj walked up to him and patted him lightly on the shoulder.

Manish opened his eyes and looked at Raj.

"Hi Raj, what're you up to these days?"

Raj gestured at Manish to follow him outside the bar. Manish put his bottle down and stood up with some effort. He had already emptied one bottle and was almost done with his second.

There was a ruckus outside the bar. A man in a *ganjee* and dirty trousers had drunk so much that he could barely stand, and two of his friends, still relatively sober, were trying to get him inside an auto rickshaw. The man, however, was in no mood to leave the bar. The driver of the autorickshaw was getting impatient and was threatening to leave. He was getting increasingly doubtful if his passenger would be able to pay for the ride.

Raj lighted two cigarettes and passed one on to Manish. They smoked silently for a minute, taking in the spectacle unfolding before their eyes.

Manish turned towards Raj and asked, "Tell me, what is the secrecy all about?" There was a smile at the corner of his lips.

"Manish bhai, we're planning an *action*."

"*We?* Who're you working with?"

"Nidhi."

"I see, your bitch!" Manish punched Raj in the belly. Both men laughed.

A truck sped along the road, blowing a cloud of dust. The dry wind played with Manish's unkempt hair. "Who's the party?" he asked.

"A *maaldaar* woman in Sri Nagar. She lives there alone with her mother and her daughter."

"What about her husband?"

"He stays in Pune."

"Sounds like an easy prey!"

"Yes, Manish bhai. Nidhi has a foolproof plan. The lady knows her. She has invited her to her house to discuss a business partnership."

"What do you want from me?" Manish asked, taking a long drag of his cigarette, his eyes narrowed. "Sounds like the two of you are sorted."

"I want you to come with us."

"Are you saying that the two of you won't be able to handle those women?" Manish laughed.

"Manish bhai, I don't want to take any chance. What if one of those women manages to escape and call the police?"

Manish nodded. Then, he asked, "When are you planning the action?"

"Tomorrow, Manish bhai. If possible."

"Fine by me. Let me know when and where we would meet."

"Thank you so much, Manish bhai. I will call you once Nidhi and I finalize the plan."

"Anything else?"

"Bhai, we need arms. A *katta*, and a couple of knives. We may not have to use them, but I want to make sure that we are prepared, in case we have to!"

"Don't worry. Those can be arranged." Manish dropped the cigarette butt to the ground and stomped on it with his chappal. He patted on Raj's shoulder and said, "Will you now let me finish my drink? The beer must have gone flat. Buy me another, will you?"

On 19 June 2011, Nidhi appeared for an examination in Betma. On completion of the test, she went home to have lunch in her house at Devendra Nagar. All along, Nidhi was calm, unperturbed by her evil plan for the afternoon.

Raj and Manish, in the meantime, had met at Rajendra Nagar. They were supposed to meet Nidhi around half past two in the afternoon near a petrol pump in Mahunaka. The two men had been drinking. Nidhi had asked Raj to save some liquor for her as well. She had already called up Mridula and set up an appointment in her house at Sri Nagar to discuss the job. The unsuspecting woman had promptly shared with Nidhi her address and the directions to her house.

The plan had been well laid out. The three would meet at Mahunaka, from where Nidhi would go to Mridula's house on her scooty, while the men would reach Sri Nagar separately on a stolen motorbike which Manish had arranged for. Nidhi would get in and start the discussions with Mridula. Then, she would call Raj on some pretext or the other. Raj and Manish would then enter the house. Raj would carry a pistol, while Nidhi and Manish would carry a knife each. They would scare

Mridula with the pistol and force her to hand all her jewellery and money over to them. The three would then run away with the loot. They would not use arms, unless forced to.

When Nidhi rang the bell, Mridula opened the door and let her in with a broad smile.

Nidhi had consumed whiskey and beer to soothe her nerves, and to silence her conscience. The cocktail was beginning to kick in.

Nidhi and Mridula sat down in the living room. Mridula began to explain to Nidhi how the seller network functioned. Nidhi kept nodding, her smile intact, as she began to feel her adrenaline pumping.

When Mridula had finished explaining the process to her, Nidhi said, "It'll be a privilege to work with you, ma'am." Out of the corner of her eye, she looked at the papers Mridula had laid out on the coffee table in front of her.

Just as Nidhi had expected, Mridula picked up a form and handed it to Nidhi. "Read this form carefully. I'll need your signature in a few places that I've marked out on the form." Mridula paused and then added, "Would you like to have something to drink? Tea or coffee?"

Nidhi turned down her offer with a smile. She read a couple of lines and then said, "Ma'am, would you mind if I call my boyfriend to also take a look? He works close by."

Mridula thought for a few seconds and then said, "Sure, call him. Let's make sure we all clearly understand the terms of the contract."

Nidhi made the call.

The whiskey spreading like venom in his veins, Raj had been waiting for Nidhi's call with bated breath. He picked up the call after the first ring.

As soon as Mridula opened the door on hearing the bell, Raj stormed into the room, Manish in tow. Manish immediately shut the door behind them. Raj pulled out his country-made pistol and pointed it at Mridula.

"If you open your mouth, I'll shoot," he slurred, his breath reeking of cheap liquor. His bloodshot eyes and the gun pointed at her head sent a wave of chill down Mridula's spine, but she tried to put up a brave front. She turned towards Nidhi and said, "Leave my house along with your friends right now, or else I will call the police."

When you have filled yourself with liquor and you have a gun in your hand, you stop using your brain. Raj pulled the trigger of his pistol in a flash. The bullet entered the side of Mridula's skull, and she collapsed to the ground like a rag doll, her scream muted forever. Nidhi jumped up from her seat, her eyes fixed on Mridula's gaping and lifeless eyes and the blood that smeared her face.

"Serves you right, bitch!" Nidhi kicked Mridula's lifeless body and looked at Raj, who was sloshed and barely in his senses. He laughed hysterically even as Anushka and Rukmini rushed to the living room on hearing the gunshot. Anushka screamed as soon as she saw her mother sprawled on the living room floor in a pool of blood. Rukmini sat down on a chair, her lips trembling.

Raj raised the gun at them and drawled, "No one opens her mouth or else I shoot! Where do you keep the money and the jewellery?"

Rukmini pointed at a cupboard in the adjoining bedroom with her hand trembling. Nidhi ran into the room. She opened the cupboard. There was a safe inside, which was locked.

"Where are the keys to the safe?" Nidhi shouted from inside the room.

Anushka walked in gingerly, her muffled sobs the only sound in the house. Raj followed her, pointing the gun at the back of her head. She pulled a drawer and handed the key over to Nidhi.

Nidhi unlocked the safe. There were wads of cash and boxes of jewellery inside. Nidhi started loading them into a bag that she found inside the cupboard. Anushka stood frozen to the spot, tears rolling down her cheeks.

Suddenly, the three were startled by Rukmini's feeble shout for help in the living room. "Help!" she cried out.

Nidhi turned towards Raj and said, "What the fuck are you waiting for? Go, shut the old hag up!"

Raj turned around, pointing the gun at the old woman a few feet away. He pulled the trigger, but the pistol betrayed him when he had least expected it to. The damn thing did not fire! Nothing unusual for a '*desi* katta', just bad timing!

Raj ran towards Rukmini, planning to throttle her neck and silence her. As luck would have it, the pistol fired just as Raj had brought his hand down. The bullet hit him straight in the foot. He screamed and sat down on the floor.

By then, Manish had caught hold of Rukmini from behind. In one quick swipe of his knife, he made a deep cut right across Rukmini's throat. The blood came gushing out, and Rukmini collapsed to the floor, silent, convulsing, her end imminent.

"*Naani!*" Anushka screamed and rushed towards her grandmother. Dropping the bag, Nidhi went after Anushka. "Fucking bitch!" she cried as she grabbed Anushka from behind by her hair. With the knife that she was carrying, Nidhi slit open Anushka's throat in a split second. The blood spurted out, and the girl fell down on her knees.

Raj and Manish kept stabbing Anushka and Rukmini for the next few minutes, as if they were possessed, as Nidhi went back to the cupboard. She had already emptied the safe. She now rummaged through the cupboard for anything else of value. When she found two ATM cards, she picked them up as well.

One by one, she then sat next to the corpses of the three ladies and removed the ornaments they had been wearing, while humming her favourite tune. Her dreams were finally going to be fulfilled. It had been a good day!

❖

After Manish had left, Nidhi took Raj to a dispensary.

She walked into the doctor's chamber and said, "Doctor, this is an emergency! My friend has been shot by some miscreants, and he needs immediate treatment!"

The doctor took a long, hard look at Raj. He examined the wound and said to Nidhi, "Madam, firstly, this is a bullet wound. You must first register a police complaint. Secondly and more importantly, you need to take your friend to a hospital. The bullet has gone too deep, and I will not be able to remove the bullet here in my clinic."

Raj went to the Annapurna police station and filed a complaint claiming that some unidentified miscreants had shot at him. Nidhi then, took Raj to a private hospital.

When the police broke into the house in Sri Nagar, they were greeted by the gruesome sight of a gory blood fest, which was unprecedented. They had not seen anything like that in their lives in the force. Some of them felt giddy, some started retching.

The area was cordoned off. The forensics experts and photographers were called in. The police spoke to the neighbours who could not be of much help. The police found that the safe had been emptied, which suggested that the murders had been committed for robbery. They also found fingerprints all over the place, and two empty shells. It was estimated that, the robbers had decamped, with one-and-a-half lakh in cash and jewellery worth five lakhs, along with two ATM cards.

When the post-mortem and forensics reports came in, there were two interesting revelations.

Firstly, a single bullet was found in Mridula's skull. The police, however, had found two shells in the house. What happened to the second bullet?

Secondly, a set of fingerprints collected at the scene of crime matched with those of Raj Malhotra, whom the Indore police had arrested earlier on a few occasions for petty crimes. The police, therefore, inferred that Raj had been involved in the robbery. An alert was issued across the city and a manhunt was initiated. Roadblocks were put up. Bus terminals, train stations and airports came under vigil. But, there was no trace of Raj Malhotra.

As for the mystery of the missing second bullet, the police came up with several theories. They had explored all the possibilities and had failed to make headway, when the officer in charge hit upon the idea that one of the robbers might have been injured during a scuffle. That was not uncommon in such incidents, where the robbers frequently fought among themselves over the sharing of the loot. The officer immediately ordered the team to check in hospitals and nursing-homes across the city, if anyone had been admitted with a bullet injury over the past forty-eight hours. It was then just a matter of time before the net closed in on Raj.

Around the same time, the police got another lead, when they were notified by the bank of multiple failed transaction attempts with the ATM cards of the Deshmukhs. Those were the same ATM cards that Nidhi had stolen.

Before long, Nidhi and Raj were nabbed by the Indore police. Acting on the information provided by Nidhi, the police arrested Manish the same evening. The loot was also recovered, as were the weapons.

In the course of the interrogation, while Nidhi admitted to being part of the gang that robbed and murdered the Deshmukhs, the wily woman that she was, she said that she had not killed any of the women.

"I was busy gathering the loot while the women were being ruthlessly slaughtered by my partners," said Nidhi, trying to distance herself from the gruesome murders.

On 13 December 2013, two-and-a-half years after their heinous crime, Nidhi, Raj and Manish were sentenced to death by the district court. It was unanimously agreed that Nidhi had been the mastermind behind the crime.

It was the first time that a woman was given capital punishment by the Indore District Court and another precedent was set by the single court by awarding death to three people in the same case.

Acting on the fifty-eight-page chargesheet filed by the police, the court said that the verdict was based on as many as ninety-six circumstantial evidences put forward by the prosecution, as well as the testimony of thirty-six witnesses.

The court in its verdict described the crime as 'rarest of the rare', identifying Nidhi as the mastermind behind the deadly plan which ended the lives of three women belonging to three generations for quick monetary gains. The verdict stated, "For the greed of some rupees, three hapless women of a family were killed in a very cruel manner. The culprits deserve no mercy."

In 2014, the Indore bench of the Madhya Pradesh High Court upheld the judgement of the district court. It was again for the first time that the High Court had upheld capital punishment for a female accused in Madhya Pradesh.

In an interesting turn of events, two years after she had been convicted, while Nidhi was in jail in death row, she received a national award on International Women's Day. While in jail, Nidhi had learned and taught the art of Zardouji. Apart from that, she had also been sharing her knowledge on personal hygiene with other female inmates.

She may have been paving her way to redemption. One can only wonder!

The Law in Her Hands

24 November 2018

It was a busy Saturday evening at Bangaliyana, the new upmarket restaurant in New Town that served traditional Bengali cuisine.

Ranjan Kumar Dutta, a Kolkata High Court lawyer, was a regular at the restaurant. The manager of the restaurant knew him by face, and so did the rest of the serving staff. Ranjan was accompanied by his wife Arpita Dutta who was a lawyer herself, and practised in both Kolkata and Mumbai High Courts. The head of the waiters welcomed them with a broad smile and led them to a table in a corner of the restaurant, which had been reserved for them.

Arpita had sent their one-and-a-half-year-old son Rehan to her parents' place in Barahanagar, along with their pet dog Bozo. The couple had the night to themselves.

They were promptly attended to by a waiter. Ranjan looked at the menu card and placed the order for dinner. Arpita, engrossed in her mobile phone, was simply nodding or uttering monosyllables in agreement with Ranjan's choices. The waiter departed after noting down the order and assured Ranjan that he would try his best to serve the food as quickly as possible, the Saturday night crowd notwithstanding.

Ranjan looked at his wife sitting across the table. She was still busy with her phone, sometimes smiling, sometimes typing messages, completely oblivious of the presence of the man in front of her.

Ranjan looked around and saw families and couples dining together, chatting and laughing heartily. He felt lonely, even in the company of his wife. It seemed to him that he had come to dine by himself.

"It seems you are busy," Ranjan finally broke the silence that sat heavy at the table.

Arpita did not look up from her phone. Ranjan cleared his throat and repeated, this time a tad louder.

Arpita looked up and asked, "Are you talking to me?"

"Well, I don't know about you, but I don't see anyone else at this table," Ranjan scoffed.

"Save the sarcasm!" Arpita said. "Yes, something urgent has come up."

"You could have told me. I would have cancelled the reservation."

Arpita kept her phone down and looked squarely at Ranjan, "Why?"

"What's the point of going out for dinner when you don't have the time to talk?"

Her phone buzzed a couple of times. Those were more messages that demanded her attention.

Arpita picked up her phone and said, "What's there to talk? That's what we do all day, anyway. Aren't we here for the food?"

The young couple at the next table took a selfie.

"I was under the impression that we would spend some quality time together; just the two of us." Ranjan smiled dryly and said, "But it seems the guy on the phone is more important for you."

Arpita put the phone down with a thud. Her face was flushed.

"Of course, this is entirely my fault now! *I* am the one who's not there for you as I am on the phone with another man!" she spoke in an angry voice.

"There you go! Now you are the victim. I am the one who's not being fair," Ranjan replied.

"Of course! You are sick, Ranjan. Stop thinking that I'm having a bloody affair. You're all screwed up inside your brain."

"Can you deny that you're having an affair?" Ranjan bent forward and pounded on the table. "You did this to your second husband when we started dating, and now you're doing the same to me. You are living a double life!"

"I can't believe this! I never thought you'd stoop so low." Arpita looked at Ranjan, stunned. "You know what, Ranjan? It's your male ego; your weak, fragile male ego that's speaking right now."

"It's not about my ego, Arpita. It's about your morals," said Ranjan. "I can't say that I wasn't warned."

"You know what?" Arpita opened her purse and dropped her phone inside. She pushed the chair back and stood up, saying, "I've had enough of this nonsense, Ranjan. I simply can't put up with this anymore. You need help. You're imagining things and making our lives miserable."

The waiter, in the meantime, had arrived with the drinks and finger food.

Arpita walked past him. She turned around and said, "Enjoy the fucking dinner, Ranjan! Thanks for the lovely evening."

She stormed out of the restaurant.

25 November 2018

The morning mist still hung low on the empty stretches of green. In the skyscrapers that had sprung up here and there by the desolate roads of New Town, there was barely any perceptible stirring of life. Most of the apartments were empty. Those living in the rest were yet to move out of the cosy warmth of their blankets.

The police were on their way to the apartment of Ranjan Kumar Dutta. They had received a call from his father Subir Kumar Dutta a while back. The father, in turn, had received a call earlier in the morning from Arpita.

"Can you please come down to our apartment as soon as you can?" Arpita had sounded panicky on the phone.

"What's the matter, Arpita? Is everything alright?" Subir Dutta had sat up straight, his heart already pounding.

"Ranjan has injured himself," Arpita had paused to breathe and had said, "I'm afraid he isn't looking good."

Subir had not wasted more time on the call. He had got dressed and had left immediately for Ranjan's apartment in New Town. Subir lived in North Kolkata. The roads would be empty at this hour of the day. It should not take him too long.

Subir stood in front of Ranjan's apartment, his hand reaching for the calling bell. That was when his eyes went to the door. To his surprise, he saw that the door was ajar. With his pulse racing, Subir pushed the door open. With his legs shaking, Subir walked in gingerly.

"Arpita!" he called out, realizing immediately that he was barely audible. "Arpita!" he called out for his daughter-in-law again. There was no reply. It seemed that, by some sinister magic, all the occupants of the apartment had vanished into thin air. The deafening silence of the empty apartment was ominous. In spite of the morning chill, there were beads of sweat on Subir's forehead. He reached out to the wall for support as he tottered towards the living room. It seemed to Subir that he would take forever to walk the few steps from the main door to the plush living room of the Dutta's.

When he reached the living room, Subir's legs gave away and he landed on the floor a few feet away from where his son was lying still. "Ranjan, Ranjan!"

Subir called out a few times, but a voice inside him told him that there would be no response. Still sitting on the floor, Subir dragged himself to his son. He brought a trembling hand near Ranjan's nose and held it there for what seemed like an eternity with the hope that if he kept his hand there long enough, he would feel the warmth of his son's breath. But that was not to be.

Thirty-four-year-old Ranjan Dutta was dead.

As the realization hit him hard, Subir's eyes widened and his jaws dropped. Getting up on his legs with a lot of effort, Subir looked around. The apartment was empty. Arpita was missing. So were Rehan, his grandson, and their dog Bozo.

With trembling hands, Subir fished out his phone and called the police.

The officer sat on a knee in front of Ranjan's body and looked at it closely. He had already sent for the forensics team and a doctor. Some of his men were checking every nook and cranny of the apartment. The rest were knocking on the doors of the neighbours.

He looked up from the body in front of him when he heard a voice behind him, "We've found his wife, sir. She was in a neighbour's flat."

The officer stood up.

Arpita was in her mid-thirties. She looked devastated, with her hair dishevelled and her eyes swollen.

"Please accept my condolences," said the officer to the grieving widow. He saw Arpita's lips move, but her words failed her.

"What is your full name, please?"

"Arpita… Arpita Dutta," the lady replied in a feeble voice. Her eyes welled up and she hid her face in her palms. The officer gave her the time to regain her composure.

"Mrs Dutta, I believe you are a lawyer yourself," the officer said. He had spoken to Subir Dutta earlier.

Arpita nodded and said, "In Kolkata High Court, as well as in Mumbai High Court."

"Who called your father-in-law?"

"I called him in the morning."

"Why did you leave the flat, Mrs Dutta?"

"I… I was scared… I didn't know what to do… I couldn't stay here…" Arpita broke down.

"Is there anyone else who lives with you in this apartment?"

"It was just the two of us last night. We have a son, Rehan; he is one-and-a-half years old. And a dog, Bozo. They are with my parents."

"In that case, I assume that it was you who found your husband in this condition."

Arpita nodded in affirmation.

"Why didn't you take your husband to a hospital?" asked the officer.

"I... I found him lying on the floor. He must have injured himself or had a cardiac arrest. I examined his body only to realize that he was no more. There was no point taking him to a hospital," Arpita said between sobs.

There was silence in the room for a while. The city was waking up. There were distant sounds of cars speeding down the New Town roads. The officer nodded and stood up.

The forensics team and the doctor arrived and conducted preliminary investigations. The body was taken away for post-mortem.

The investigating officer had the post-mortem report of Ranjan Dutta in front of him. His brows were creased as the implications of the report began to sink in.

The report claimed that Ranjan had died due to the choking of his windpipe, and that there was a ligature mark on his neck. It was also suggested that Ranjan might have been beaten up before his death. There were injury marks on both sides of Ranjan's head.

Arpita Dutta was summoned again for interrogation.

"Mrs Dutta, we have the post-mortem report of your husband, and it is proved beyond doubt that he did not die of a cardiac arrest, or, for that matter, any injury that he might have sustained that night."

Arpita lowered her head and ran her tongue over her parched lips.

"Would you mind telling us what really happened inside your apartment on the night of 24 November?" the officer asked, raising his voice a notch higher.

Arpita looked up, startled. She then, lowered her head again and said slowly, "Yes, officer. Ranjan did not die a natural death. *He committed suicide.*"

The officer sat up straight. "You knew it all along and yet you had been lying to us?" he asked.

"Yes... yes, officer. I was too scared to divulge the truth."

"Tell me what happened that night. Don't leave out any detail," the officer said sternly.

Arpita began her story.

"We had gone out for dinner that night; just the two of us. As I told you earlier, Rehan was with my parents. It was quite late by the time we returned home after dinner. Ranjan was tired and wanted to go to bed. I had a few calls to make and wanted to be by myself in the other bedroom."

"Who did you want to call?" the officer interrupted Arpita, "You said just now that it was quite late in the night."

"I wanted to call my friends," said Arpita. The officer did not miss the hesitation in her voice. "And we had a fight," she said.

"A fight? What did you fight over?"

"You see," Arpita said hesitantly, "Ranjan was insecure and suspicious. He used to get all worked up if I even talked to another man. That night, we had a showdown. He started hurling abuses at me, using the filthiest of words. I refused to give in. You see, officer, I had had enough. My self-respect had taken a beating. There was no way I was going to sleep with him in the same room. Then, Ranjan started threatening me."

"How did he threaten you?"

"He said that he would kill himself if I spent the night in the other bedroom."

"Had he threatened you in the past as well? Or, was that the first time?" the officer asked.

"He would always blackmail me emotionally with suicide threats, officer. That was nothing new."

The officer nodded and said, "So, you moved to the other bedroom with your phone, I assume."

"I did."

"What happened next?" he further enquired.

"I don't remember the exact time, but there was a power cut and the lights went out. I woke up. I wanted to check out what was wrong, and I stepped out of my room. I stepped into the living room. It was dark and..." Arpita closed her eyes.

The officer waited patiently till Arpita resumed.

"I saw him sitting on the floor. At first, I thought he must also have woken up because of the power cut. I called him by his name, but he did not answer. I thought he was still mad at me and wouldn't talk to me. But, when I went closer to him, I realized that there was something weird about his posture. I bent down to look closely and saw that there was a bedsheet wrapped around his neck!" Arpita's voice quivered. She paused briefly and continued, "I pushed him gently and he just dropped to the floor. He was dead! He had... he had hanged himself from the ceiling."

"What did you do next?"

"I was so frightened when I figured out that Ranjan had killed himself! I ran away to a neighbour's flat."

"I am certain my son has not committed suicide. He was murdered."

That was Subir Dutta's reaction when the police asked him if he believed Arpita's statement that Ranjan had hung himself. "I am confident that there has been foul play," Subir kept repeating himself.

However, the police were not so sure. Ranjan Dutta was five feet eight inches tall and weighed nearly ninety kilograms. Was it possible for a woman to single-handedly hang him from the ceiling of their living room? Was there a third person in the house that night? The police decided to recreate the scene using a dummy.

The next day, Subir Dutta lodged a murder complaint against Arpita and three other members of her family – her father Ashok Das, mother Sarbari Das, and her brother Anik Das. The fact that Arpita had been married twice in the past did not help her case in the media trial.

The investigating officer went back to Arpita's statement and considered it in the light of the post-mortem report, as well as the report from the forensics laboratory.

The contradictions now stared him in the face.

Ranjan Dutta's post-mortem report mentioned that he might have been strangulated with a fine thread as the ligature mark around his neck was not very prominent. The nature of the ligature suggested the use of something like a thin wire or a silk string for strangulation. Ranjan had not been asphyxiated by a thick bedsheet wrapped around his neck, as Arpita had claimed. The forensic doctors also corroborated this in their report.

Although the recreation at the crime scene had been inconclusive, the police were certain that without the help of an accomplice, it would not have been possible for Arpita to hang Ranjan from the ceiling. This added further credence to the theory that Ranjan might have been strangulated with a thin wire, and had not been hung from the ceiling.

While the police had initially believed that Ranjan had indeed committed suicide, one of the heads of the Bidhannagar commissionerate, in charge of the case, was sceptical. Three other observations strengthened the theory of murder.

Firstly, the fact that the son and the dog had been bundled away to Arpita's parents' house before that night. Was that a mere coincidence? Or was it done on purpose to keep the child and the pet away from the scene of crime?

Secondly, Arpita had made no effort to take Ranjan to a hospital that morning. The police found out that Arpita had first called her father-in-law Subir Dutta and then, she had called her brother Anik. Anik had not bothered to call the police on receiving Arpita's call. He had not taken Ranjan to a hospital either. Did Anik know that Ranjan had already died?

Finally, the inconsistencies in Arpita's statements were glaring. She had initially claimed that Ranjan had hurt himself. She had then, stated that Ranjan had experienced a cardiac arrest. When her earlier statements had been challenged with the post-mortem report, she had claimed that Ranjan had committed suicide and that she had been aware all along but had been 'afraid' to divulge the truth.

There were also several inconsistencies in terms of timelines, circumstances and sequence of events. There had been around six different versions of Arpita's statement in a very short span of time. There was a strong possibility that Arpita, a lawyer herself, had been trying to confuse the police and to find procedural loopholes.

Arpita was detained on the morning of Saturday, 1 December. The head of the commissionerate, along with some of his colleagues, grilled Arpita for more than eight hours.

Arpita finally broke down and confessed that she had indeed killed her husband.

"Yes, yes! I killed him! I strangled him with the cord of my mobile charger, and then wrapped a bedsheet around his neck to make it look like he had killed himself."

"You are a lawyer, Mrs Dutta! Didn't you realize that the cause of death would be revealed in the post-mortem report?"

"I knew that the cause of death would be revealed as asphyxiation. But I thought that the ligature made by a thin wire, like that of the cord of a mobile phone charger, would be so faint that it would not be detected. I thought that it would seem that Ranjan had died from asphyxiation caused by the bedsheet wrapped tightly around his neck."

"I have to say, it was your bad luck, Mrs Dutta! The ligature, though not very prominent, was detected during post-mortem, and it was clear that Mr Dutta had not been killed by the bedsheet," the head of the commissionerate paused briefly and then asked Arpita, "For how long had you been planning the murder?"

"It was an act of impulse and not a pre-mediated murder," she replied. "Ranjan would routinely torture me, both physically and mentally. He would regularly threaten me with committing suicide and getting me arrested on abetment charges. He had started abusing and threatening me on Saturday night as well. We had an argument and I strangled him with the cord of my mobile charger on impulse."

"Why did you not confess earlier?"

"I was worried about my son. He is just a year-and-a-half old. He needs me."

The questions kept coming, one after another.

"You are a lawyer yourself. If you've been a victim of serial domestic abuse, why didn't you act on it earlier? You could have dragged your husband to court."

"If your strangling Ranjan was an act of impulse and you didn't really mean to kill your husband, why didn't you try to save him? Why didn't you take him to a hospital?"

"Was it a mere coincidence that you sent your son and your pet off to your parents' house in advance?"

None of Arpita's responses, however, sounded convincing.

Late in the night of 1 December, the then Deputy Commissioner, Detective Department of Bidhannagar City Police, informed the media that after the day-long interrogation, Arpita had been arrested. One of the officers in charge of the investigation, while speaking to the media, said, "At first, we thought it was a suicide. But soon enough, I started thinking deeper. It seemed Arpita should be grilled further, as there were inconsistencies in her answers. The truth came out only after that."

The police also seized Arpita's mobile phone and laptop to study her call lists and social media activities. In the upcoming months, electronic evidence would come to play a critical role in the investigation. In fact, the case was closely observed by the Supreme Court of India and turned out to be one of the earliest cases in the country, where digital and electronic evidences played a key role in the delivery of justice.

The police verified the CCTV footages of the restaurant where Arpita and Ranjan had had dinner on the night of the incident. It was revealed that the couple had left the restaurant separately, possibly after an argument.

Over the next several weeks, shocking details began to surface from Arpita's WhatsApp conversations and Facebook activities.

It became evident from an analysis of Arpita's WhatsApp conversations that, contrary to the carefully created veneer of marital bliss, her marriage with Ranjan had hit rock bottom. Their relationship had come to a virtual end several months before Ranjan's death. Among other reasons, Arpita was not happy with Ranjan's financial situation. She had been contemplating divorce for a long time. However, Ranjan had not been willing to end his marriage, mainly due to his apprehensions about the future of their son. Arpita would often abuse Ranjan physically.

The police found out from WhatsApp conversations that the couple often fought over the length of time that Arpita routinely spent on the phone, and over the long calls that she would frequently make to her male friends. They had also had an argument on the night of Ranjan's death over the same issue. She had assaulted Ranjan on the night of the murder as well. That explained the head injuries which the post-mortem report had mentioned.

The investigating team correlated this observation with Arpita's earlier statement where she had claimed that she had wanted to be alone in the bedroom on the fateful night. The couple had fought bitterly over that. The police did not rule out the possibility of an extramarital affair being the reason behind the murder.

Arpita's Facebook page was a study in contrasts.

Just days before Ranjan's death, Arpita had been posting pictures and videos of how the family had been enjoying themselves during the Durga Puja festival in Kolkata. There were pictures of the couple dining out on the evening of Maha Shashthi. There was a video of Arpita dancing with a *dhunuchi* to the rhythm of the *dhaak*. There were pictures of Arpita with her husband, her forehead smeared with sindoor, on Bijaya Dashami, the last day of the Durga Puja festivities. She had mentioned in the caption that she was looking forward to the Puja festivities next year.

Just days before his death, commenting on one of Arpita's posts, Ranjan had written:

> *I believe our love is immortal. And it's only for us. By God's grace, we do not need to show it off on social media. We do not need to keep telling each other 'I love you like anything', 'Love you Jaanu/Honey' and things like that. All I want to say is, stay the same forever. Stick around with me till my last breath.*

At the same time, some of Arpita's posts on Facebook were shocking.

In one of her posts dated 7 November, Arpita had compared marriage to a 'public toilet', those waiting outside were dying to get in and those inside could not wait to get out. Arpita had the habit of extensively searching on Google and then sharing on Facebook links to news reports detailing different cases where women had murdered their husbands.

In a chilling observation, the police saw that in a post dated 22 November, just three days before allegedly killing her husband, Arpita had shared the link of a story where a woman had murdered her husband, chopped the body into pieces, cooked Biryani with the meat and fed it to a mason working in the house.

One certainly needs guts of steel to look up, enjoy and share stories of this nature!

More incriminating evidences were unearthed from Arpita's browsing behaviour. In addition to looking up stories where women had brutally murdered their husbands, Arpita's Google searches were mostly about finding information on strangulation techniques. In fact, a few hours before Ranjan's death, Arpita had Googled the phrase 'ligature materials'. Looking at the links that Arpita had visited thereafter, the police could easily figure out that she had got the idea of using the cord of a mobile phone charger right there. Her search history also revealed that Arpita had thoroughly studied how a murder could be passed off as a suicide.

Within eighty-one days, Bidhannagar Police submitted the chargesheet for the case of the murder of lawyer Ranjan

Dutta at Barasat Court. Arpita Dutta was named as prime suspect. The chargesheet, however, did not include the names of Arpita's brother and her parents, who had earlier been accused by Ranjan's family.

The police presented digital evidences, thirty-two medico-legal witnesses, audio enhancements, photography enhancements, forensic video analysis and digital enhancements of latent fingerprints.

In March 2019, Arpita's advocate appealed for bail on the grounds that the entire case was based only on circumstantial evidences and the police had not produced an 'iota of evidence' against Arpita, a respectable practising advocate. She had a suckling baby and had already been in custody for more than hundred days.

However, prosecution argued that, the *modus operandi* for the murder was evident. Just before the murder, Arpita had removed the child and the pet dog from the apartment. The murder, therefore, appeared to be a premediated one. The mobile charger, the cord of which had been used for strangulating the victim, had been seized from the flat and had been identified by Arpita. If Arpita was released on bail, there were chances of tampering of evidence and influencing witnesses, most of whom were her neighbours.

The bail plea was rejected by the court.

In September 2020, the Barasat court found Arpita Dutta guilty under IPC Sections 302 (committing murder) and Section 201 (causing disappearance of evidence of offence). She was sentenced to life imprisonment.

Interestingly, this verdict marked one of the earliest examples of the admissibility of electronic digital evidence in criminal prosecutions in India. Speaking to the media, the public prosecutor said, "This was a unique investigation. The evidence filed before the court was based almost entirely on the convict's mobile call, chat and Google search history."

Ranjan's family was disappointed with the verdict as they had expected nothing short of a death sentence for Arpita. Arpita, on the other hand, shouted at media persons as she was being taken to the police van, claiming that she had been wrongly framed by the police and her son's future had been jeopardized by the court. She resolved to appeal to the higher court and 'fight for justice till the last drop of her blood'.

The Habitual Murderer

The lush greenery and the smell of damp soil in the air are warm invitations for the lazy and idyllic lifestyle of the sleepy town of Koodathayi, with its population of less than twelve thousand, located in the Kozhikode district of Kerala.

The pastel-pink three-storey house of the Varghese family – with its iron fence and an iron gate, its balcony lined with ornate and white balustrades – stands out amidst the modest dwellings of their neighbours and the dense, green jungle all around. A small plaque on the gate bears the name of John Varghese, the man who built the house.

In the predominantly Muslim town, the Vargheses belonged to the small community of Christians. Dolly Varghese, the daughter-in-law of the late John Varghese, was the pillar of the community. Fondly called 'Dolly teacher' by her neighbours, Dolly was respected by everyone in the small town as a distinguished academician. An active member of the Roman Catholic community, Dolly was described as friendly, jovial and pious by those who knew her. She stood by her neighbours whenever they were sick or in trouble.

"This house is cursed," poor Dolly would often lament to her neighbours. She had every reason to think that way. Her mother-in-law, Anna Varghese, had died from a mysterious illness shortly after Dolly had become a part of the Varghese family by marrying Roger Varghese, the eldest of the three children of Anna and John. Her father-in-law, John, had died a few years later. Dolly had lost her husband shortly thereafter. Two more of her relatives had suffered fatal heart attacks and her eighteen-month-old niece had choked on a snack.

But, Dolly was a devout Christian, and her faith in the power of the almighty only seemed to grow as destiny inflicted one wound after another on her tormented soul.

Dolly and Roger met at a housewarming party, and it was love at first sight. Roger, a trader by profession, fell for Dolly's charm and wit. As he got to know Dolly better, Roger loved her even more, for her kind and loving nature and her willingness to serve and help those in need.

Roger's father John Varghese had retired as a clerk in the State Education Department and his mother, Anna Varghese, was a teacher. Anna was the life of the house. In addition to her work in the school, she took care of the house and her family, tutored children and frequently hosted lavish dinners for her family and friends. The Varghese family was famous for their annual Christmas party, which was the biggest in the town, where all their neighbours were invited.

Dolly and Roger got married in July 1997. Anna took an instant liking to the pretty and caring girl her son had married.

"Roger has found a girl who's not only beautiful, but has a university degree! I couldn't have asked for a better match for my son. She's the right choice for our family," Anna would proudly tell her neighbours.

"You must study further and find yourself a job. A woman must not spend her entire life caught up in domestic chores." Those were Anna's words of advice for her daughter-in-law. Anna was a progressive and liberal woman and wanted the women in the house to stand on their own two feet.

On Anna's insistence, Dolly completed her Bachelor of Education course. Anna had retired in the meantime, and Dolly started working as a guest lecturer in St. Thomas College in the town of Pala. Roger and Dolly had been blessed with two sons by then, but Dolly managed to visit her kids only on weekends. After a while, Dolly started teaching in the National Institute of Technology, Kozhikode. That way, she could stay with her family and travel for work daily. Dolly was happy with the job and would proudly show off her identity as a 'professor' in National Institute of Technology,

Kozhikode, that bore the institution's motto, "*From darkness, lead us into light.*"

Despite her long workdays, Dolly always managed to find the time to help Anna and Rebecca, her sister-in-law, with cooking and domestic chores. She led a prayer group in the community. She also went to church every Sunday, arriving early enough so that she could grab one of the front pews. Before long, she became a sister to Rebecca, and Anna would often ask her own daughter to learn from Dolly.

Little did the family realize that their days of bliss were numbered.

Anna had been unwell for a while and Dolly had been taking care of her. On the morning of 22 August 2002, when the old lady collapsed, frothing at the mouth, she was immediately taken to the town hospital, where she was declared dead.

Anna's death seemed to have snuffed the life out of the Varghese house. There was a pall of gloom all around. The regular visits by friends and family became few and far between. The Christmas parties grew smaller with every passing year, and finally stopped altogether. John, who loved his wife dearly, became a recluse. The grieving old man rarely spoke to his children. He was also saddened by the growing dispute among his children – Roger, Robert and Rebecca – over the possession of his property.

John passed away in 2008, six years after the death of his wife. On the fateful day, Mohammed, a neighbour, heard someone continuously vomiting next door. Before long, he received a call from Dolly.

"Mohammed, can you come over please? John is very sick, and there's no one else at home," Dolly pleaded on the phone. She sounded panic-stricken. When Mohammed reached the house, he found John lying on his back, convulsing and foaming at the mouth. "We must take him to the hospital immediately," he said.

When Dolly and Mohammed took John to the town hospital, the doctors declared that the sixty-six-year-old had already died from a heart attack.

After John's death, the dispute over his property intensified. Roger produced a will that named him as the sole inheritor of his father's fortune. However, the will neither had a date, nor the signatures of witnesses which was why it was declared invalid.

Three years later, on the night of 30 September 2011, tragedy struck the family once again.

Mohammed had just finished his dinner, when he received Dolly's call.

"Dolly, is everything alright?" there was genuine concern in Mohammed's voice.

"Mohammed, I'm sorry to bother you so late. But I think there's something wrong with Roger. Can you come over, please?" Dolly's voice shook as she spoke.

Mohammed arrived at the Varghese residence in no time. Dolly was waiting for him at the gates.

"Roger is in the washroom for quite some time now! I've been cooking dinner and calling out for him repeatedly. But he's not answering," Dolly explained as they ran up the stairs. "I've also been banging on the door, but he refuses to come out!" Dolly added, trying hard to get a grip on herself.

"Who else is in the house?" Mohammed was already climbing two steps at a time.

"There's no one else at home," Dolly said, trying to catch up with Mohammed. "I'm not feeling too well about this!"

Mohammed banged on the washroom door and called out Roger's name a few times, but there was no response. Before long, Mohammed was joined by a couple more neighbours, and the washroom door, which had been locked from inside, was broken down. Roger was found lying on the floor of the toilet, unconscious, foaming from the mouth – a crude reminder of the deaths of his parents. Dolly cried out, her guttural wails echoing in the empty house.

Roger was rushed to the town hospital where he was declared dead due to a massive heart attack. The family was shattered. However, Mark, one of Roger's uncles, insisted on an autopsy.

"Roger was a healthy young man, and I find it very hard to believe that he would suffer a heart attack out of the blue!" Mark said in a family gathering. He lowered his voice and told Dolly who was sitting next to him, "I am also mindful of the ongoing dispute among the siblings over John's property. I would advise you to get an autopsy done."

Therefore, an autopsy was carried out, and, just as Mark had apprehended, traces of cyanide were detected.

Dolly, however, was not willing to accept that someone in the family had poisoned her husband. With teary eyes, she said to the police, "I don't believe that anyone in our family would do this to Roger. Everyone loved him." With some hesitation, she added, "Of late, Roger had been going through a financial crisis and had been depressed. He had also started drinking heavily. He must have, somehow, got hold of the cyanide and ended his life."

The police did not probe further and the case was closed. It was rather unusual that the police did not bother to find out where the cyanide had come from.

A year later, in 2012, a new will of John Varghese surfaced, naming Roger Varghese as the sole inheritor of his property. It bore signatures of witnesses who were not known to the rest of the Varghese family. It was a valid will, nevertheless.

Now that Roger was dead, Dolly inherited the entire family fortune. But, she was just a shadow of her old self. She became withdrawn and barely socialized. Despite all that, she was a regular at the church, and was actively involved in charitable activities of the community. The neighbours empathized with the young widow and allowed Dolly her space.

In 2014, Mark passed away. Dolly had visited him around half past three in the afternoon to check if he had had lunch, as his wife had been away on that day. Seeing that Mark was unwell, Dolly alerted the neighbours. Mark died before he could be taken to the town hospital.

Roger had a cousin named Stephen Xavier. The Xaviers were very close to the Varghese family. Stephen was a high school teacher who was highly respected in the community. He had experienced his share of grief. His daughter Rosy, an eighteen-month-old toddler, passed away after choking on a snack on the morning of her brother's communion in May 2014. Two years later, in 2016, he lost his wife Sarah to an epilepsy episode.

Stephen and Dolly had immense love and respect for each other. Destiny had left both of them alone, mercilessly snatching from them their near and dear ones. In 2017, a year after Sarah's death, Stephen married Dolly.

Dolly still visited the cemetery where Roger and his family had been buried to put flowers and light candles on their graves. She still made sure that she did not miss the Sunday mass. Her kindness and devotion made Stephen fall deeply in love with her.

Rebecca and Robert, however, were far from happy and the property disputes between Dolly and her first husband's siblings continued unabated. In January 2019, Rebecca filed a lawsuit to contest the ownership of a plot of land. As part of the proceedings of the lawsuit, Rebecca gained access to the post-mortem report of her brother, Roger, for the first time. As she went through the post-mortem report, she noticed a glaring discrepancy. The hair on her neck stood up.

She had to call her brother, Robert. She looked at the watch. It was quite late in the USA, where Robert presently lived. However, this could not wait till tomorrow. Rebecca reached for the phone.

❖

"What the..." Robert muttered groggily as his phone rang on the nightstand. He picked it up and looked at the name of the caller. "Rebecca? Is everything fine?" Robert sounded alarmed. A call at an odd hour scared every Varghese, after everything the family had gone through over the last few years.

"Robert, I am sorry to wake you up, but there's something you must know. It's about Roger."

Robert was wide awake in seconds.

"I've been going through Roger's post-mortem report and something doesn't quite add up. You know as well as I do that Dolly has always regretted that Roger died on an empty stomach, even while she had been cooking dinner for him. She keeps harping on this, doesn't she? However, the post-mortem report says quite the opposite! It clearly mentions that Roger died within minutes of eating a dinner of rice and chickpea curry. You know how much Roger loved chickpea curry! Dolly would often prepare his favourite dish for him."

"What are you trying to say?" Robert asked as his throat went dry. Rebecca did not miss the tremor in her brother's voice.

"Robert, all I am asking is – why did Dolly lie?"

❖

A few weeks later, Robert returned to Kerala. When Rebecca and Robert confronted Dolly with the discrepancies in the post-mortem report, she stuck to her original story. In fact, the entire Varghese family took offence and accused the siblings of trying to stir up trouble, just when Dolly had found love and peace after a long time. The family felt that the siblings were trying to create chaos just because they had their eyes on John's property, which rightfully belonged to Roger, and after his untimely demise, to Dolly.

However, their suspicion now fuelled, the siblings began to make enquiries about Dolly.

"Where do you think we should start?" Rebecca asked her brother.

"We need to figure out who those two witnesses of John's will were. No one from the extended family knew them. They could be Dolly's friends. I want to start from Dolly's workplace," Robert said. He already had a plan.

What Robert came to know at the National Institute of Technology, Kozhikode left him stunned.

Dolly Varghese had never worked there. For seventeen long years, Dolly had been making an hour-long commute daily, supposedly to the institute in Kozhikode. Where had she really been going?

Robert and Rebecca summoned Mohammed, and the three started going over the details of the deaths in the family all over again, right from the death of Anna in 2002.

"Mohammed, you live right next door. You've known our family for years. In fact, you were with Dolly when John and Roger died. Anna, John, Roger, Mark – they all died identical deaths! Doesn't this strike as odd to you?" Robert asked Mohammed, trying to throw light into the dark chambers of his memory.

Mohammed remained silent for a few minutes, trying to put his finger on what exactly had been bothering him subconsciously over the years. He finally said, "I've always thought that it was a strange coincidence. *Not only had Dolly been present during all the four deaths in the Varghese family over the last seventeen years, but she had also been alone with the deceased every time.*"

The penny dropped. The silence inside the room was deafening.

After a while, Mohammed said, "You know what? *Dolly had also been present during the two deaths in the Xavier family!*"

Robert's eyes widened. He was quiet for a few seconds, trying to assimilate the information he had just received. Then, he asked Mohammed, "Are you saying, Dolly was around when Stephen's baby died?"

"Yes. Dolly had been invited to Stephen's house on the day of his son's communion, when Rosy died from choking on her food," Mohammed said.

"What about Sarah's death?" Robert sounded restless.

"Sarah and Stephen were returning from a wedding along with Dolly that evening," said Mohammed.

Robert looked at Rebecca and said, "We must not lose any more time. It's now on us to deliver justice to everyone Dolly has killed ruthlessly over the years!"

Robert and Rebecca lodged a complaint with the district police chief of Kozhikode, and eventually, a police report was filed. The siblings raised their suspicion about the mysterious circumstances in which six members of their family had died over the last seventeen years. They suspected that all six members of the family had been murdered. The district police conducted preliminary investigations. When they were convinced of the merit of the case, they filed a report before the Deputy Inspector General of Police, Kannur Range, and a Special Investigating Task Force was put together in August 2019. Six different teams were created to probe the six alleged murders, with a supervisory team to coordinate the activities of the teams. Forensic and legal experts were inducted into the task force.

The biggest crime investigation in the history of Kerala Police was flagged off.

"The case is a very challenging one as there is a gap of fourteen years between the first and the sixth alleged killing. The challenge, in this case, is that the first murder took place seventeen years back, and the last one took place three years back. Therefore, the collection of evidence is most crucial," said the Chief of Kerala Police.

Like Robert, the police also found out from the registrar of the National Institute of Technology at Kozhikode that Dolly had never worked there. It turned out that she had only visited the campus and had tea in the canteen on a few occasions.

As there had been no post-mortem on the bodies, apart from that of Roger Varghese, the police decided to exhume the bodies for forensic investigations. On 4 October, the police first opened the vaults in St Mary's Church, where Rosy and Sarah had been buried. The burial vaults in Lourde Matha Church were opened next, where John, Anna, Roger and Mark had been buried. Forensic investigations continued through the day.

"I just pray that we can bring my family members justice. You don't know what it does to me, as a daughter and a sister, to see the remains of my loved ones taken out from their graves after such a long time," said Rebecca Varghese.

On 5 October 2019, forty-seven-year-old Dolly Varghese was arrested as the prime suspect for six murders in the Varghese and Xavier families, sending shock waves through the small town of Koodathayi. "She couldn't have done this! There must've been a mistake!" Those were the words on everyone's lips.

When the police started interrogating Dolly, she dodged their questions skilfully. The police, in the meantime, had found out that Dolly had several powerful and well-connected friends, two of them being seasoned advocates. They must have coached her on how to wriggle out of a police interrogation.

When questioned about the deaths of her parents-in-law, Dolly put the blame on her deceased husband saying, "You know what, officer? I've always wondered if it was Roger who killed Anna and John and forged a will to gain sole possession of John's property."

However, the police pointed out the circumstances of Anna's death in 2002, and also produced the list of persons who had been present in the Varghese house on that day, according to accounts of eyewitnesses. That list did not include Roger. Similarly, on the day of John's death in 2008, Dolly had been the only one present in the house. Mohammed had also told the police that it was Dolly who had called him up, asking for help.

When Dolly realized that she had her back to the wall, she confessed with an air of indifference that she had killed her parents-in-law, Anna and John.

The police found the bottle of cyanide, wrapped in clothes and hidden among old utensils, during a search of the Varghese house. Dolly had allegedly got the cyanide from a friend, Michael, who, in turn, had procured it from a goldsmith, Prem Kumar. Goldsmiths are legally allowed to buy cyanide, which is used in the processing of gold, but it is illegal for them to sell it. Michael and Prem were arrested by the police.

When the police started interrogating Dolly about the death of her husband Roger, stressing on the fact that the autopsy had found cyanide in his body, Dolly looked coldly at the officer and said, "I've said this before, and I will say this again. It's very likely that Roger killed himself. We were quickly running out of money, and he had been depressed for months."

"Let me remind you, however, that Michael and Prem have confessed to supplying the cyanide that killed Roger," the officer said.

"Well, that doesn't make any difference. Michael might have given the cyanide to Roger, and in fact, abetted the act of suicide, as he might have had a personal enmity with Roger. You should be asking him, not me," Dolly said.

"Let me then inform you that we've found out that Michael had been out of town for days leading up to Roger's death, and on the day itself. There is, in fact, no evidence in support of your allegation. Michael has told us that he had passed on the cyanide to you, on your request, before Roger died," the officer dealt the final blow.

Dolly had no option left but to confess that she had indeed murdered her husband, Roger.

By the time the police completed their interrogation, Dolly had confessed to killing all six members of the Varghese and Xavier families.

"You know, I always kept the cyanide handy to kill myself, in case I was caught. But I've never had to take the poison in seventeen long years, through half-a-dozen murders! I was destined to own all this wealth, and live happily with Stephen, the love of my life. But, I guess, there comes a time when god's kindness runs out," Dolly said.

As the investigation progressed, more and more shocking truths were unravelled.

Dolly's early years

Dolly, a first-year dropout in college, wanted to impress Roger and her would-be in-laws with her academic qualifications. She, therefore, claimed that she had obtained Bachelor's and Master's degrees in Commerce, and forged copies of certificates to support her claim. Believing her, Anna wanted her daughter-in-law to continue with her studies and start working. To evade Anna's regular reminders, Dolly went back to her native town and on return, claimed that she had completed her B.Ed course. Thereafter, she lied to her family about her jobs at St. Thomas College and later, at National Institute of Technology, forging identity cards of the institutions.

Dolly confessed to the police that she had been to Chennai and Coimbatore eleven times on the pretext of attending trainings for teachers. In reality, the purpose of the visits was to see plots of land, buy clothes and jewellery, and enjoy the company of her many male friends.

Murder 1: Anna Varghese, 2002

Dolly was unhappy over the fact that Anna had complete control over the family finances. Dolly's ambition to gain control over the financial dealings of the family, coupled with the stress Dolly was subjected to because of Anna's constant enquiries about her education and employment, prompted Dolly to plan Anna's murder.

"Nothing will make me happier than to be able to take care of you, Anna," Dolly told her mother-in-law when she fell sick in August 2002. "You take care of me like my own mother would. Now, it's my turn."

She acquired a prescription for 'Dog Kill' – a poisonous substance used for killing diseased dogs – from the Government Veterinary Hospital at Kozhikode. She used the fake name Dolly Devagiri and purchased the poison from a chemist at Kozhikode.

On the morning of 22 August 2002, Anna was under the weather. "Let me take care of the chores. You get some rest, will you?" Dolly urged her mother-in-law, adding, "I will make you a warm bowl of mutton soup. You'll feel better in no time!"

The soup was laced with the poison that took Anna's life. Because Anna had already had health issues, her death was not considered unusual, and there was no post-mortem conducted.

Within three days of Anna's death, her gold ornaments and her personal diary went missing. Before long, Dolly took complete control of the family's finances.

That was the first step that Dolly took towards establishing herself as the unquestioned matriarch of the Varghese family.

Murder 2: John Varghese, 2008

After Anna's death, the dispute over John's property among his children intensified.

"You must put the house in the name of Roger and myself," Dolly demanded of her father-in-law.

"I can offer you a lump sum amount from the sale of the paddy field. It's a two-acre land, and the money is good. However, let me make this clear, Roger would then have no right over the rest of my property. I will divide it between Rebecca and Robert," John said in no uncertain terms.

Dolly realized that she would never gain complete ownership of the property with John around. She meticulously planned John's murder.

In 2008, Dolly procured cyanide from Michael, a relative who worked in a jewellery shop and with whom she had struck a friendship, claiming that she needed the poison to kill rats in the house. Michael, in turn, got the cyanide from Prem Kumar in exchange for two bottles of alcohol and five thousand rupees. Michael had not mentioned to Prem Kumar that the cyanide was meant for Dolly. Instead, he had told Prem that he needed the poison to kill a rat. Michael was unaware of Dolly's evil plan and handed the poison over to Dolly.

Dolly poisoned John's food with the cyanide.

She had, in the meantime, also managed to forge a will. Roger produced that will after his father's death, but the will was deemed invalid as it had neither a date nor the signatures of witnesses.

Murder 3: Roger Varghese, 2011

Roger looked at the wall clock as Dolly walked in through the door.

"Where have you been all evening?" he screamed at her.

"There was a meeting in college after classes got over," Dolly replied, without bothering to look at Roger, as she walked towards the washroom.

"Why don't you tell me the truth? Who have you been fucking?" Roger lost his temper. He had come to know that Dolly had been sleeping around.

Dolly stopped in her tracks and turned towards Roger.

"You know what? I'm tired of your disgusting suspicions. I work in a college. I work for the community. I meet a lot of people. I do have friends, and some of them happen to be men. That doesn't mean I sleep around," Dolly paused briefly and then continued, "Look at you! You are stupid and narrow-minded. Your mind is filled with superstitions. You're running out of money and you've hit the bottle in frustration. How dare you point fingers at me?"

Roger ran his fingers through his hair and said, "Yes, you are right! I'm a fool. I didn't recognize you. You are an evil woman who hides her true self behind a façade of innocence, kindness and charm, which manages to fool the entire village. Those idiots love you. They respect you. But, all you can think of is how to gain possession of the family property and how to fulfil your sexual needs. Your mind is full of shit!"

"Okay, why don't you leave me then?" Dolly asked with a smirk.

"I would right now if I could. But, I worry about the future of my sons and I don't want to bring disrespect to the Varghese family. That's why I drown my sorrows in my drink."

Roger walked into his room and shut the door behind him.

As she stood under the shower, Dolly reflected on her situation. With an elaborate plan for gaining possession of the family property already laid out, Dolly now wanted a man who was financially stable and was of a liberal and progressive nature. Roger's cousin, Stephen Xavier, fit the bill perfectly. She had been eyeing him for a while now.

The first step in that direction, however, was to eliminate Roger.

One night, she mixed cyanide with the rice and chickpea curry she had cooked for her husband. Roger went to the washroom after dinner and never came out alive.

Within a year, Dolly produced a forged will with signatures from two of her male friends as witnesses. The police, during the investigation, found out that Dolly's brother-in-law Danny might have helped her forge the will to take over the Varghese family property. Robert felt that Dolly had friends in the right places, and he did not rule out the possibility that she had been helped by government officials to forge the documents.

Murder 4: Mark Varghese, 2014

When Roger passed away under mysterious circumstances, Mark suspected foul play, especially because the siblings had been embroiled in a dispute over John's property. It was on his insistence that an autopsy was conducted, where it was revealed that Roger had died from cyanide poisoning.

Dolly managed to handle the 'crisis' by convincing the family that Roger had committed suicide by consuming cyanide, as he had become a depressive alcoholic. But, for the next two years, Mark kept demanding a police investigation into Roger's death. He wanted to challenge the will which awarded sole inheritance of John's property to Roger, and after his death, to Dolly.

It had, however, not occurred to Mark that Dolly herself might have been the mastermind behind all the deaths in the family. Dolly played a masterstroke by befriending Mark, instead of opposing his demands for police investigation. They became drinking partners. A retired soldier, Mark always had a steady supply of alcohol. He even gifted liquor bottles to Dolly.

"You are such a nice girl, Dolly! It's such a shame that Roger's brother and sister ganged up against him and you," Mark would say in his drunken stupor, "But, don't worry! I'll get to the bottom of this. No one gets away with murder!"

Dolly knew that she would have to eventually eliminate Mark, as he was a genuine threat, determined to unravel the mystery behind Roger's death. One fateful afternoon, when

Mark's wife was away, Dolly joined him for a drink. She laced Mark's drink with cyanide and killed him.

Murder 5: Rosy Xavier, 2014

After the death of Roger Varghese, Dolly wanted to marry Stephen. She was attracted to him because of his calm and liberal demeanour, as well as by the fact that he earned a steady salary from the government as a teacher. However, Stephen was dedicated to his family. Dolly knew that he would not leave them to marry her. It was, therefore, important to get Stephen's family out of the way.

The Xavier family was celebrating the first communion of Abel, who was Stephen's elder son, on 1 May 2014. Dolly had been invited to the Xaviers' residence.

It was around half past nine in the morning, and Sarah, Stephen's wife, was caught up in the rituals. It was time to feed the baby.

"Let me take care of your princess," Dolly told Sarah with a warm smile, cuddling her eighteen-month-old daughter, Rosy. "It's Abel's special day. Be with him."

Dolly fed Rosy a meal of bread and meat curry, laced with the cyanide, which she had procured from Michael. The little girl collapsed immediately after consuming the food. Stephen took his daughter to the town hospital, and from there, to two more hospitals with the hope of better treatment, but all his efforts were in vain. Rosy passed away on 3 May, without responding to treatment.

Stephen's darling daughter was out of the way. Next, it was Sarah's turn.

Murder 6: Sarah Xavier, 2016

As Sarah grieved the death of her daughter, Dolly got friendlier with her husband. Stephen also seemed to have taken a fancy for the young widow. Sarah was unhappy about the situation. Dolly realized that Sarah had to be eliminated next, if she were to carry out her plan of marrying Stephen.

Dolly kept looking for an opportunity and found one when the three of them went together to a family wedding. On their way back, Stephen dropped by a dentist's clinic, as Sarah and Dolly waited for him outside. The heat was sweltering, and Sarah was thirsty.

"I wonder how much longer he's going to take," Sarah said, as she wiped her brow with her handkerchief. "I'm thirsty."

Dolly heard her and immediately reached inside her bag for a bottle of water. Sarah did not notice the devilish glint in her eyes.

"Here, have some water," Dolly passed the bottle on to Sarah.

Little did Sarah know that the water had cyanide mixed in it. Dolly had been anxiously waiting for an opportunity all day to get Sarah to drink from that bottle.

Sarah collapsed and landed on Dolly's lap as soon as she drank the water. She died before Stephen could take his wife to the hospital. Sarah had a history of epileptic attacks and her death was attributed to a heart attack brought about by an epilepsy episode.

Dolly and Stephen got married the very next year, in 2017.

Other suspected murders

The police, on further investigation, found out that Dolly might have been involved in other murders or attempted murders in the Varghese family.

Dolly might have tried to murder Rebecca in 2002, a few months after Anna's death. Rebecca had shown signs of uneasiness after drinking an ayurvedic tonic, which had been given to her by Dolly. Rebecca had been wise to drink plenty of water. She told the police that she had not suspected foul play at the time, but now that Dolly had confessed to the cold-blooded murders of six persons from the Varghese and Xavier families over a period of fourteen years, Rebecca might have been on her hit-list as well.

Relatives raised doubts about the mysterious deaths of two more men from the Varghese family, Suresh and Vivian. They were both John Varghese's nephews. Vivian was found dead in his house under mysterious circumstances in 2002, days after Anna's death. Suresh died in a bike accident in 2008. Relatives later found Suresh's personal diary. He had scribbled Dolly's name in several pages. In one of the pages in the diary, he had written that 'he had been cheated'.

When one commits a murder and gets away with it, a switch flips inside. Henceforth, for every problem that life throws one's way, the only solution one can think of is to take another life. Killing becomes a habit. That, precisely, was the case with Dolly Varghese.

"While I want justice to take its own course, I would remain strong for the sake of my brother," said Remo, Dolly's eldest son. "However, I think it is unlikely that my mother alone carried out all the murders. Stephen was probably an accomplice, at least in the murders of his first wife and child. What surprised me was the fact that Stephen appeared unperturbed by their deaths. He does not treat my brother and me well, either."

Sarah's brother had also suggested that Stephen might have been involved in the murder of his sister. The police, therefore, grilled Stephen for several hours in course of the investigation.

Stephen claimed that Dolly and her son were trying to implicate him in her heinous acts. "I have not had the faintest idea about Dolly's secrets. I did not know that Dolly did not work in the National Institute of Technology. Likewise, I did not know that the autopsy conducted on Dolly's first husband back in 2011 had revealed traces of cyanide in his body," said Stephen.

"We've been told that the deaths of your first wife and child did not affect you much," the investigating officer tried to provoke Stephen. Provocation was often the best instrument to unearth hidden truths.

Stephen smiled dryly and said, "On the contrary, officer, the deaths of my daughter and my first wife in quick succession left me shattered. Dolly was pressurizing me for marriage. I requested her to wait for a year."

"What about reports in the media that Dolly had two abortions after her marriage with you? Is that true?"

Stephen looked sharply at the officer and said, "I did accompany Dolly to a gynaecologist on three occasions, but every time, I was asked to wait outside, and I have no idea what transpired inside the clinic."

Later, the police let Stephen off with strict travel restrictions, as they did not find any concrete evidence against him.

In February 2020, Dolly tried to commit suicide inside the Kozhikode district prison by using a sharp object. There were three other inmates in the cell with Dolly. They alerted the warden immediately. Dolly was admitted first to the district hospital and then to Kozhikode Medical College Hospital.

All through the year in 2020, as the world came under the grip of the COVID pandemic, Dolly languished in jail and appeared in multiple court hearings through video conferencing.

The prosecution lined up close to two hundred and fifty witnesses, to prove the allegations against Dolly, Michael and

Prem. The witnesses included close relations of Dolly and the Varghese family members.

Her defence counsel tried to prove that on account of the dispute over the Varghese property, Robert had brought false allegations against Dolly, and that she had been falsely implicated by the investigating agency.

However, Dolly's bail applications, barring the one pertaining to the case of the murder of Anna Varghese in 2002, were rejected on the ground that the witnesses included her children and her neighbours. There were possibilities of her influencing or intimidating them if she was released on bail.

In February 2021, the Supreme Court of India also stayed Dolly's release from custody.

Today, the Varghese's house, for which Dolly took the lives of her husband, her parents-in-law, and an uncle, stands in a dilapidated condition. The iron gates have gathered rust. So has the lock that hangs on them. The driveway and the walls are covered with thick moss. The locals believe that the house is cursed, which is why they stay away from it after dark. Most of the neighbours claim that they have heard strange noises inside the house in the night. Some of them have seen ghostly figures roaming around in the balconies.

Dolly's children live with Rebecca now. After everything that the family had gone through, she decided to start afresh with rekindled energy and spirits, building her new family. But whenever Dolly's name comes up in any conversation, she never hesitates to express herself.

"If I were to meet Dolly, I would thank her for sparing her two sons. They are now my children. At least, I could save them from the monster. They are my blood," Rebecca tells everyone she meets. She had finally left the baggage of the past behind and moved on with pride.

Epilogue

Dev had stayed up all night and studied seven of the most shocking cases that Professor Dutt had shared with him. He stretched his arms and walked to the window adjacent to his study desk with a steaming cup of black coffee in his hand. The sky was clearing up and it was the beginning of a new day.

The meeting with the professor and then going through the case files had completely changed Dev's perspective on women criminals. Those were women associated with some of the most violent crimes committed in the country in the last few decades. For him, criminality and violence had always been synonymous with masculinity, mostly because of the power and the aggression that he naturally associated with such acts.

While women have taken huge strides in every profession, the lens through which they are viewed, especially in a country like India, is still that of motherhood. So, when a woman commits an act of violence, it challenges our notion of womanhood. We, therefore, have a tendency to dismiss these acts as aberrations, instead of accepting the fact that the female of the species is as much, if not more, capable of violent crimes as the male.

Just as Dev was heading for the washroom to freshen up, the newspaper landed in the balcony with a thud. He picked it up and started looking cursorily at the headlines on the front page, when a news item at the bottom grabbed his attention.

A woman had been arrested in Kolkata after she had allegedly smashed her son's head with a grindstone and roasted his body with camphor and spices in what apparently was a tantric ritual. The semi-charred skeleton had been dumped on the terrace of a house in the Salt Lake area of Kolkata. Earlier, the police had launched an investigation for a missing person based on a complaint filed by the woman's estranged husband. He had not been able to contact his son for a while.

It turned out that the woman had started practising tantra, which had soured her relationship with her husband. He had moved out of their house and had started living separately. Their elder son suffered from multiple ailments related to heart, food pipe and neurological disorders. The woman had decided to sacrifice him for some tantric rituals for the betterment of the fortunes of her family. The police found a big *kadhai* (cauldron) in which the son was set on fire with ghee, camphor and spices to conceal the stench of burning flesh.

Dev dropped the paper on the desk and reached for the phone, his hand still shaking from the effect of the shocking news. He had to call up the professor and discuss the case.

It was not just lust and greed that drove women to commit heinous acts of violence. Blind faith was a powerful motivation as well!

Did the professor know about more such cases?

References

1. Wife listens over phone unfazed even as her lover kills husband | Kolkata News – *The Times of India* – https://timesofindia.indiatimes.com/city/kolkata/wife-listens-over-phone-unfazed-even-as-her-lover-kills-husband/articleshow/58726349.cms
2. Wife gets husband killed, hears his shrieks over phone as lover beats him to death – https://newsable.asianetnews.com/india/wife-gets-husband-killed-hears-his-shrieks-over-phone-as-lover-beats-him-to-death
3. Police found new evidence on Anupam Sinha murder case – *Anandabazar* – https://www.anandabazar.com/state/police-found-new-evidence-on-anupam-sinha-murder-case-1.616325
4. Manua, Ajit granted life term; parents of Anupam dissatisfied – *Millennium Post* | *DailyHunt* – https://m.dailyhunt.in/news/

india/english/millennium+post-epaper-millpost/manua+aji t+granted+life+term+parents+of+anupam+dissatisfied-newsid-127421706

5. Woman, lover accused of killing former's husband convicted by Bengal court – India News – *Hindustan Times* – https://www.hindustantimes.com/india-news/woman-lover-accused-of-killing-former-s-husband-convicted-by-bengal-court/story-iZxQqS0NRXJ5FcDkH9nkHN.html#:~:text=A%20district%20court%20in%20Bengal,fast%20track%20court%20in%20Barasat.
6. Anupam Sinha News in Bengali, Videos & Photos about Anupam Sinha – Anandabazar.com – https://www.anandabazar.com/topic/anupam-sinha?ref=story-stry-tag
7. Manua's maternal uncle can not believe about her character – *Anandabazar* – https://www.anandabazar.com/state/manua-s-maternal-uncle-can-not-believe-about-her-character-1.617464
8. Ajit murdered Anupam because Manua did not want to waste money for a contract killer – *Anandabazar* – https://www.anandabazar.com/calcutta/ajit-murdered-anupam-because-manua-did-not-want-to-waste-money-for-a-contract-killer-1.617460?ref=hm-new-stry
9. Manua has Murderer mentality, Police says at Charge Sheet – *Anandabazar* – https://www.anandabazar.com/district/24-paraganas/manua-has-murderer-mentality-police-says-at-charge-sheet-1.655200
10. Investigators believe that Manua Majumdar may have some other motives behind the murder – *Anandabazar* – https://www.anandabazar.com/calcutta/investigators-believe-that-

manua-majumdar-may-have-some-other-motives-behind-the-murder-1.616893

11. Bengal woman 'plots husband's murder, wanted to hear him scream in agony' – Kolkata – *Hindustan Times* – https://www.hindustantimes.com/kolkata/bengal-murder-woman-wanted-to-hear-husband-s-shrieks-as-her-lover-beat-him-to-death/story-vWlSY08nGyqbmqb1t6B50N.html
12. This Woman Used Her Lover To Kill Husband, What Happened Next Will Blow Your Mind – *The Male Factor* (TMF) – https://themalefactor.com/2017/05/27/this-woman-used-her-lover-to-kill-husband-what-happened-next-will-blow-your-mind/
13. Indian Kanoon: Ranadhir Basu vs State Of West Bengal on 24 September, 1998 – *Indian Kanoon* – http://indiankanoon.org/doc/632451/
14. Indian Kanoon: Ranadhir Basu vs State Of West Bengal on 7 February, 2000 – *Indian Kanoon* – http://indiankanoon.org/doc/406498/
15. Indian Kanoon: Ram_Singh_vs_Sonia_&_Ors_on_15_February,_2007 – http://indiankanoon.org/doc/1384369/
16. Poonia murders – Wikipedia – https://en.wikipedia.org/wiki/Poonia_murders
17. Ex-MLA family clubbed to death – *Telegraph India* – https://www.telegraphindia.com/india/ex-mla-family-clubbed-to-death/cid/922945
18. *The Tribune*, Chandigarh, India – Main News – https://www.tribuneindia.com/2001/20010825/main4.htm
19. *The Tribune*, Chandigarh, India – Main News – https://www.tribuneindia.com/2004/20040601/main2.htm

20. They killed 8 of their own, then spent 12 years in uncertainty | India News, *The Indian Express* – https://indianexpress.com/article/india/india-others/why-these-15-were-spared-death/
21. Killer Sonia's sapna was money money – https://mumbaimirror.indiatimes.com/news/india/killer-sonias-sapna-was-money-money/articleshow/15682217.cms
22. rediff.com: Sonia confesses to having killed her father, 7 family members – https://www.rediff.com/news/2001/aug/26har.htm
23. Know about Sonia, Sanjiv facing the death noose in Haryana for killing 8 family members – https://www.indiatvnews.com/crime/news/know-about-sonia-sanjiv-facing-the-death-noose-in-haryana-for-killing-family-members-3018.html
24. Death to daughter for killing family | *Hindustan Times* – https://www.hindustantimes.com/india/death-to-daughter-for-killing-family/story-MBxpIsh0UhudNXHVSyFVXJ.html
25. Let me die, says woman on Death Row for killing 8, Govt tells President show no mercy – *Indian Express* – http://archive.indianexpress.com/news/let-me-die-says-woman-on--death-row-for-killing-8-govt-tells-president-show-no-mercy/468634/0
26. They murdered entire families for land, loot or revenge – *Indian Express* – http://archive.indianexpress.com/news/they-murdered-entire-families-for-land-loot-or-revenge/1103529/0
27. Pranab clears way for first-ever hanging of a woman – *The Hindu* – https://www.thehindu.com/news/national/pranab-clears-way-for-firstever-hanging-of-a-woman/article4585676.ece

28. Sonia and Sanjiv hanging fixed for November 26 – *Oneindia News* – https://www.oneindia.com/2007/09/08/sonia-and-sanjiv-hanging-fixed-for-november-26-1189245781.html
29. Slain Haryana legislator Relu Ram Phogat's son-in-law jumps parole – *The New Indian Express* – https://www.newindianexpress.com/nation/2018/jun/13/slain-haryana-legislator-relu-ram-Phogat%E2%80%8Bs-son-in-law-jumps-parole-1827331.html
30. Relu Ram murder convict attempts suicide in jail : *The Tribune* India – https://www.tribuneindia.com/news/archive/haryana/relu-ram-murder-convict-attempts-suicide-in-jail-673698
31. Relu ram murder convicted Sonia attempt to suicide in jail – https://www.jagran.com/haryana/kurukshetra-relu-ram-murder-convicted-sonia-attempt-to-suicide-in-jail-18569252.html
32. 'She wanted this house, it's now a graveyard' – *Indian Express* – http://archive.indianexpress.com/news/-she-wanted-this-house-its-now-a-graveyard/468635/0
33. Indian Kanoon: Jollyamma Joseph @ Jolly vs The State Of Kerala on 20 March, 2020 – https://indiankanoon.org/doc/60815150/
34. Indian Kanoon: Jollyamma Joseph vs State Of Kerala on 15 October, 2020 – https://indiankanoon.org/doc/37539924/
35. Jolly's motive was to gain ancestral property: report – *The Hindu* – https://www.thehindu.com/news/national/kerala/jollys-motive-was-to-secure-ancestral-property-report/article29964617.ece
36. Koodathayi murders: How the dark hues of a criminal mind unfolded | Kerala News | *English Manorama* – https://www.

onmanorama.com/kerala/top-news/2019/10/08/koodathayi-morders-story-so-far.html

37. Police Say Cyanide Soup and 6 Deaths Point to a Serial Killer – *The New York Times* – https://www.nytimes.com/2019/10/19/world/asia/india-koodathayai-murder.html
38. Jolly Joseph: Mom, churchgoer, chatty neighbor ... suspected serial killer – *CNN* – https://edition.cnn.com/2019/11/08/asia/jolly-joseph-murder-india-intl-hnk/index.html
39. Kerala serial killer Jolly: Everything you need to know | India – *Gulf News* – https://gulfnews.com/world/asia/india/kerala-serial-killer-jolly-everything-you-need-to-know-1.1570526945036
40. Jovial, friendly, pious: Shocked Kerala town recalls its 'serial killer' who killed 6 people over 14 years | India – *Gulf News* – https://gulfnews.com/world/asia/india/jovial-friendly-pious-shocked-kerala-town-recalls-its-serial-killer-who-killed-6-people-over-14-years-1.1570461633045
41. Two bottles of alcohol & Rs 5,000: How co-suspect in Koodathayi murders got cyanide| Kerala News | *Manorama English* – https://www.onmanorama.com/kerala/top-news/2019/10/14/koodathayi-murder-jolly-cyanide-mathew-prajikumar-statements.html
42. Koodathayi Cyanide Murders – Wikipedia – https://en.wikipedia.org/wiki/Koodathayi_Cyanide_Murders
43. Koodathayi serial murders: Jolly cosied up to Mathew before killing him in first bid | Kerala News | *Manorama English* – https://www.onmanorama.com/news/kerala/2019/11/08/jolly-mathew-manjadiyil-murder-motive-koodathayi-serial-killing.html

44. Alleged serial killer Jolly Joseph attempts suicide in jail, hospitalised | *The News Minute* – https://www.thenewsminute.com/article/alleged-serial-killer-jolly-joseph-attempts-suicide-jail-hospitalised-119014
45. Anindita Pal @ Anindita Pal Dey vs Unknown on 18 March, 2019 – https://indiankanoon.org/doc/18985063/
46. Rajat Dey Murder: How police solved the case and nabbed his wife Anindita Pal Dey dgtl – *Anandabazar* – https://www.anandabazar.com/calcutta/rajat-dey-murder-how-police-solved-the-case-and-nabbed-his-wife-anindita-pal-dey-dgtl-1.1203707
47. West Bengal: Lawyer convicted for killing husband 2 years ago | Kolkata News – *The Times of India* – https://timesofindia.indiatimes.com/city/kolkata/lawyer-convicted-for-killing-husband-2-yrs-ago/articleshow/78114425.cms
48. Lawyer who killed husband with phone charger chord gets jail for life – Kolkata – *Hindustan Times* – https://www.hindustantimes.com/kolkata/lawyer-jailed-for-life-for-suffocating-husband-with-mobile-charger-chord/story-kslnBCmntU6ar2NchGNXQJ.html
49. Wife of Calcutta High Court lawyer pronounced guilty of murdering him in 2018 – Kolkata – *Hindustan Times* – https://www.hindustantimes.com/kolkata/wife-of-calcutta-high-court-lawyer-pronounced-guilty-of-murdering-him-in-2018/story-vyOMl7PrQ80JihLQYC698J.html
50. Sentenced for life, this woman shared stories of murderous wives like her – https://www.sirfnews.com/sentenced-for-life-for-husbands-murder-anindita-pal-dey-used-to-share-on-fb-stories-of-wives-murdering-their-men/

51. Barasat Court to deliver verdict today on lawyer Rajat Dey's death case – *Anandabazar*
52. https://www.anandabazar.com/calcutta/barasat-court-to-deliver-verdict-today-on-lawyer-rajat-dey-s-death-case-1.1202390
53. Rajat Dey Murder Case: Bail application of Anindita Pal has been rejected by Court – *Anandabazar*
54. https://www.anandabazar.com/calcutta/rajat-dey-murder-case-bail-application-of-anindita-pal-has-been-rejected-by-court-1.967947
55. Charge sheet submitted in murder case of Calcutta High Court lawyer Rajat Dey – *Anandabazar*
56. https://www.anandabazar.com/state/charge-sheet-submitted-in-murder-case-of-calcutta-high-court-lawyer-rajat-dey-1.954688
57. New Town lawyer's death: Mystery deepens as wife admits to murder – http://www.millenniumpost.in/kolkata/new-town-lawyers-death-mystery-deepens-as-wife-admits-to-murder-330047
58. https://eisamay.indiatimes.com/west-bengal-news/kolkata-news/advocate-wife-arrested-in-murder-of-high-court-lawyer-rajat-dey-at-new-town/articleshow/66930445.cms
59. Police is still clueless in Lawyer Rajat Dey murder case of New Town dgtl – *Anandabazar*
60. https://www.anandabazar.com/calcutta/police-is-still-clueless-in-lawyer-rajat-dey-murder-case-of-new-town-dgtl-1.909396
61. Kolkata lawyer's wife arrested for his murder, extramarital affair suspected – India News – *Hindustan Times*
62. https://www.hindustantimes.com/india-news/kolkata-lawyer-s-wife-arrested-for-his-murder-extramarital-affair-suspected/story-YS58VwpPThcabYdOrNWtbN.html

63. Advocate wife arrested in murder of High Court Lawyer Rajat Dey at their New Town flat
64. http://www.uniindia.com/advocate-wife-arrested-in-murder-of-high-court-lawyer-rajat-dey-at-their-new-town-flat/east/news/1423558.html
65. Srinagar triple murder case Death for mastermind girl, two others – https://www.freepressjournal.in/indore/srinagar-triple-murder-case-death-for-mastermind-girl-two-others
66. Death to woman, two others for murder upheld – https://www.dailypioneer.com/2014/state-editions/death-to-woman-two-others-for-murder-upheld.html
67. https://hindi.news18.com/photogallery/crime/thriller-story-of-neha-verma-who-was-sentenced-to-three-deaths-in-triple-murder-case-of-indore-1670957.html
68. Neha verma: the inhuman face of the indore triple murder – *Daily Bhaskar* – https://daily.bhaskar.com/news/MP-IND-neha-verma-the-inhuman-face-of-the-indore-triple-murder-2214657.html
69. Indore triple murder: a few hours before the ghastly crime, mastermind neha was giving an exam – *Daily Bhaskar* – https://daily.bhaskar.com/news/MP-IND-indore-triple-murder-a-few-hours-before-the-ghastly-crime-mastermind-neha-was-giving-an-exam-.html
70. Neah Verma | Murderpedia, the encyclopedia of murderers – https://murderpedia.org/female.V/v/verma-neah.htm
71. Maria_Monica_Susairaj_vs_Malad_Police_Station_on_14_October,_2008 – http://indiankanoon.org/doc/1357102
72. 305089782-Court-Order-of-Neeraj-Grover-Murder-Trial-Mumbai

73. Neeraj Grover murder case – Wikipedia https://en.wikipedia.org/wiki/Neeraj_Grover_murder_case
74. Neeraj case: Maria gets 3 years in jail, boyfriend 10 years – *India News* – https://www.indiatoday.in/india/west/story/sentencing-in-neeraj-grover-murder-case-136631-2011-07-01
75. Maria Susairaj | Latest News on Maria-susairaj | Breaking Stories and Opinion Articles – *Firstpost* – https://www.firstpost.com/tag/maria-susairaj
76. READ: The chilling confessions of Maria Susairaj – Rediff.com India News – https://www.rediff.com/news/report/read-the-chilling-confessions-of-maria-susairaj/20110701.htm
77. Neeraj Grover killing: Maria Susairaj's confession – https://www.ndtv.com/india-news/neeraj-grover-killing-maria-susairajs-confession-460086
78. 'Case based on evidence, not Maria's confession' – https://mumbaimirror.indiatimes.com/mumbai/other/case-based-on-evidence-not-marias-confession/articleshow/16136459.cms
79. 'Maria's confession vital to prove her conduct' – https://mumbaimirror.indiatimes.com/mumbai/other/marias-confession-vital-to-prove-her-conduct/articleshow/16139305.cms
80. Susairaj claims cops forced her to confess to Grover's murder | Cities News, *The Indian Express* – https://indianexpress.com/article/cities/mumbai/susairaj-claims-cops-forced-her-to-confess-to-grovers-murder/
81. Jerome Blames Maria For Grover Murder | India News – *India TV* – https://www.indiatvnews.com/news/india/jerome-blames-maria-for-grover-murder-9206.html

82. None happy with Grover case verdict – *The Hindu* – https://www.thehindu.com/news/national/none-happy-with-grover-case-verdict/article2151334.ece
83. Maria absolved of Grover killing | *The Deccan Herald* – https://www.deccanherald.com/content/172697/maria-absolved-grover-killing.html
84. 'It took me four hours to chop body' | *Hindustan Times* – https://www.hindustantimes.com/india/it-took-me-four-hours-to-chop-body/story-AjdvD9utCbOk0Gfu0lciGJ.html
85. Kolkata: Woman and son arrested for killing elder son, burning body – https://indianexpress.com/article/cities/kolkata/woman-and-son-arrested-for-killing-elder-son-burning-body-7102810